History of Hernando Cortez

Makers of History

History of Hernando Cortez

Makers of History

JOHN S.C. ABBOTT

COSIMO CLASSICS

NEW YORK

History of Hernando Cortez: Makers of History

History of Hernando Cortez: Makers of History was originally published in 1856.

For information, address:
P.O. Box 416, Old Chelsea Station
New York, NY 10011

or visit our website at:
www.cosimobooks.com

Ordering Information:
Cosimo publications are available at online bookstores. They may also be purchased for educational, business or promotional use:
- *Bulk orders:* special discounts are available on bulk orders for reading groups, organizations, businesses, and others. For details contact Cosimo Special Sales at the address above or at info@cosimobooks.com.
- *Custom-label orders:* we can prepare selected books with your cover or logo of choice. For more information, please contact Cosimo at info@cosimobooks.com.

Cover Design by www.popshopstudio.com

ISBN: 978-1-60520-766-7

The next morning, Cortez, with a showy retinue of horsemen, prancing through streets upon which hoof had never before trodden, called upon the emperor. The streets were lined, and the roofs of the houses crowded with multitudes gazing upon the amazing spectacle. The Spanish chieftain was kindly received by the emperor, and three days were appointed to introduce him to all the objects of interest in the capital. Tenochtitlan was the native name by which the imperial city was then known.

—from "The Metropolis Invaded"

PREFACE.

THE career of Hernando Cortez is one of the most wild and adventurous recorded in the annals of fact or fiction, and yet all the prominent events in his wondrous history are well authenticated. All *truth* carries with itself an important moral. The writer, in this narrative, has simply attempted to give a vivid idea of the adventures of Cortez and his companions in the Conquest of Mexico. There are many inferences of vast moment to which the recital leads. These are so obvious that they need not be pointed out by the writer.

A small portion of this volume has appeared in Harper's Magazine, in an article furnished by the writer upon the Conquest of Mexico.

CONTENTS.

ENGRAVINGS.

HERNANDO CORTEZ.

Chapter I.

The Discovery of Mexico.

The shore of America in 1492.

THREE hundred and fifty years ago the ocean which washes the shores of America was one vast and silent solitude. No ship plowed its waves; no sail whitened its surface. On the 11th of October, 1492, three small vessels might have been seen invading, for the first time, these hitherto unknown waters. They were as specks on the bosom of infinity. The sky above, the ocean beneath, gave no promise of any land. Three hundred adventurers were in these ships. Ten weeks had already passed since they saw the hills of the Old World sink beneath the horizon.

For weary days and weeks they had strained their eyes looking toward the west, hoping to see the mountains of the New World rising in the distance. The illustrious adventurer, Christopher Columbus, who guided these frail barks, inspired by science and by faith, doubted not that a world would ere long emerge before him from the apparently boundless waters. But the blue sky still overarched them, and the heaving ocean still extended in all directions its unbroken and interminable expanse.

Discouragement and alarm now pervaded nearly all hearts, and there was a general clamor for return to the shores of Europe. Christopher Columbus, sublime in the confidence with which his exalted nature inspired him, was still firm and undaunted in his purpose.

The night of the 11th of October darkened over these lonely adventurers. The stars came out in all the brilliance of tropical splendor. A fresh breeze drove the ships with increasing speed over the billows, and cooled, as with balmy zephyrs, brows heated through the day by the blaze of a meridian sun. Columbus could not sleep. He stood upon the deck of his ship, silent and sad, yet indomitable in energy, gazing with intense and unintermitted watch into the dusky distance. It was near midnight. Suddenly he saw a light, as of a torch, far off in the horizon. His heart throbbed with an irrepressible tumult of excitement. Was it a meteor, or was it a light from the long-

AMERICA DISCOVERED

wished-for land? It disappeared, and all again was dark. But suddenly again it gleamed forth, feeble and dim in the distance, yet distinct. Soon again the exciting ray was quenched, and nothing disturbed the dark and sombre outline of the sea. The long hours of the night to Columbus seemed interminable as he waited impatiently for the dawn. But even before any light was seen in the east, the dim outline of land appeared in indisputable distinctness before the eyes of the entranced, the now immortalized navigator. A cannon—the signal of the discovery—rolled its peal over the ocean, announcing to the two vessels in the rear the joyful tidings. A shout, excited by the heart's intensest emotions, rose over the waves, and with tears, with prayers, and embraces, these enthusiastic men accepted the discovery of the New World.

The bright autumnal morning dawned in richest glory, presenting to them a scene as of a celestial paradise. The luxuriance of tropical vegetation bloomed in all its novelty around them. The inhabitants, many of them in the simple and innocent costume of Eden before the fall, crowded the shore, gazing with attitude and gesture of astonishment upon the strange phenomena of the ships. The adventurers landed, and were received upon the island of San Salvador as angels from heaven by the peaceful and friendly natives. Bitterly has the hospitality been requited. After cruising around for some time among the beautiful islands of the New World, Columbus returned to Spain to astonish Europe with the tidings of his discovery. He had been absent but seven months.

A quarter of a century passed away, during which all the adventurers of Europe were busy exploring these newly-discovered islands and continents. Various colonies were established in the fertile valleys of these sunny climes, and upon the hill-sides which emerged, in the utmost magnificence of vegetation, from the bosom of the Caribbean Sea. The eastern coast of North America had been during this time surveyed from Labrador to Florida. The bark of the navigator had discovered nearly all the islands of the West Indies, and had crept along the winding shores of the Isthmus of Darien, and of the South American continent as far as the River La Plata. Bold explorers, guided by intelligence received from the Indians, had even penetrated the interior of the isthmus, and from the summit of the central mountain barrier had gazed with delight upon the placid waves of the Pacific. But the vast indentation of the Mexican Gulf, sweeping far away in an apparently interminable circuit to the west, had not yet been penetrated. The field for romantic adventure which these unexplored realms presented could not, however, long escape the eye of that chivalrous age.

Some exploring expeditions were soon fitted out from Cuba, and the shores of Mexico were discovered. Here every thing exhibited the traces of a far higher civilization than had hitherto been witnessed in the New World. There were villages, and even large cities, thickly planted throughout the country. Temples and other buildings, imposing in massive architecture, were reared of stone and lime. Armies, laws, and a symbolical form of writing indicated a very considerable advance in the arts and the energies of civilization. Many of the arts were cultivated. Cloth was made of cotton, and of skins nicely prepared. Astronomy was sufficiently understood for the accurate measurement of time in the divisions of the solar year. It is indeed a wonder, as yet unexplained, where these children of the New World acquired so philosophical an acquaintance with the movements of the heavenly bodies. Agriculture was practiced with much scientific skill, and a system of irrigation introduced, from which many a New England farmer might learn many a profitable lesson. Mines of gold, silver, lead, and copper were worked. Many articles of utility and of exquisite beauty were fabricated from these metals. Iron, the ore of which must pass through so many processes before it is prepared for use, was unknown to them. The Spanish goldsmiths, admiring the exquisite workmanship of the gold and silver ornaments of the Mexicans, bowed to their superiority.

Fairs were held in the great market-places of the principal cities every fifth day, where buyers and sellers in vast numbers thronged. They had public schools, courts of justice, a class of nobles, and a powerful monarch. The territory embraced by this wonderful kingdom was twice as large as the whole of New England.

The code of laws adopted by this strange people was very severe. They seemed to cherish but little regard for human life, and the almost universal punishment for crime was death. This bloody code secured a very effective police. Adultery, thieving, removing landmarks, altering measures, defrauding a ward of property, intemperance, and even idleness, with spendthrift habits, were punished pitilessly with death. The public mind was so accustomed to this, that death lost a portion of its solemnity. The rites of marriage were very formally enacted, and very rigidly adhered to.

Prisoners taken in war were invariably slain upon their religious altars in sacrifice to their gods. Slavery existed among them, but not hereditary. No one could be born a slave. The poor sometimes sold their children. The system existed in its mildest possible form, as there was no distinction of race between the master and the slave.

Military glory was held in high repute. Fanaticism lent all its allurements to inspire the soldier. Large armies were trained to very considerable military discipline. Death upon the battle-field was a sure passport to the most sunny and brilliant realms of the heavenly world. The soldiers wore coats of mail of wadded cotton, which neither arrow nor javelin could easily penetrate. The chiefs wore over these burnished plates of silver and of gold. Silver helmets, also, often glittered upon the head.

Hospitals were established for the sick and the wounded.

Their religious system was an incongruous compound of beauty and of deformity—of gentleness and of ferocity. They believed in one supreme God, the Great Spirit, with several hundred inferior deities. The god of war was a very demon. The god of the air was a refined deity, whose altars were embellished with fruits and flowers, and upon whose ear the warbling of birds and the most plaintive strains of vocal melody vibrated sweetly.

There were, in their imaginations, three states of existence in the future world. The good, and especially those, of whatever character, who fell upon the field of battle, soared to the sun, and floated in aerial grace and beauty among the clouds, in peace and joy, never to be disturbed. The worthless, indifferent sort of people, neither good nor bad, found perhaps a congenial home in the monotony of a listless and almost lifeless immortality, devoid of joy or grief. The wicked were imprisoned in everlasting darkness, where they could do no farther harm.

It is an extraordinary fact that the rite of infant baptism existed among them. This fact is attested by the Spanish historians, who witnessed it with their own eyes, and who have recorded the truly Christian prayers offered on the occasion. As the infants were sprinkled with water, God was implored to wash them from original sin, and to create them anew. Many of their prayers dimly reflected those pure and ennobling sentiments which shine so brilliantly in the word of God.

Their worship must have been a costly one, as the most majestic temples were reared, and an army of priests was supported. One single temple in the metropolis had five thousand priests attached to its service. The whole business of youthful instruction was confided to the priests. They received confession, and possessed the power of absolution.

The temples were generally pyramidal structures of enormous magnitude. Upon the broad area of their summits an altar was erected, where human victims, usually prisoners taken in war, were offered in sacrifice. These awful ceremonies were conducted with the most imposing pomp of music, banners, and military and ecclesiastical processions. The victim offered in sacrifice was bound immovably to the stone altar. The officiating priest, with a sharp instrument constructed of flint-like lava, cut open his breast, and tore out the warm and palpitating heart. This bloody sacrifice was presented in devout offering to the god. At times, in the case of prisoners taken in war, the most horrid tortures were practiced before the bloody rite was terminated. When the gods seemed to frown, in dearth, or pestilence, or famine, large numbers of children were frequently offered in sacrifice. Thus the temples of Mexico were ever clotted with blood. Still more revolting is the well-authenticated fact that the body of the wretched victim thus sacrificed was often served up as a banquet, and was eaten with every accompaniment of festive rejoicing. It is estimated that from thirty to fifty thousand thus perished every year upon the altars of ancient Mexico. One of the great objects of their wars was to obtain victims for their gods.

The population of this vast empire is not known. It must have consisted, however, of several millions. The city of Mexico, situated on islands in the bosom of a lake in the centre of a spacious and magnificent valley of the interior, about two hundred miles from the coast, was the metropolis of the realm.

Montezuma was king—an aristocratic king,

surrounded by nobles, upon whom he conferred all the honors and emoluments of the state. His palace was very magnificent. He was served from plates and goblets of silver and gold. Six hundred feudatory nobles composed his daily retinue, paying him the most obsequious homage, and expecting the same from those beneath themselves. Montezuma claimed to be lord of the whole world, and exacted tribute from all whom his arm could reach. His triumphant legions had invaded and subjugated many adjacent states, as this *Roman empire* of the New World extended in all directions its powerful sway.

It will thus be seen that the kingdom of Mexico, in point of civilization, was about on an equality with the Chinese empire of the present day. Its inhabitants were very decidedly elevated above the wandering hordes of North America.

Montezuma had heard of the arrival, in the islands of the Caribbean Sea, of the strangers from another hemisphere. He had heard of their appalling power, their aggressions, and their pitiless cruelty. Wisely he resolved to exclude these dangerous visitors from his shores. As exploring expeditions entered his bays and rivers, they were fiercely attacked and driven away. These expeditions, however, brought back to Cuba most alluring accounts of the rich empire of Mexico and of its golden opulence.

The Governor of Cuba now resolved to fit out an expedition sufficiently powerful to subjugate their country, and make it one of the vassals of Spain. It was a dark period of the world. Human rights were but feebly discerned. Superstition reigned over hearts and consciences with a fearfully despotic sway. Acts, upon which would now fall the reproach of unmitigated villainy, were then performed with prayers and thanksgivings honestly offered. We shall but tell the impartial story of the wondrous career of Cortez in the subjugation of this empire. God, the searcher of all hearts, can alone unravel the mazes of conscientiousness and depravity, and award the just meed of approval and condemnation.

Many good motives were certainly united with those more questionable which inspired this enterprise. It was a matter of national ambition to promote geographical discoveries, to enlarge the realms of commerce, and to extend the boundaries of human knowledge by investigating the arts and the sciences of other nations. The Christian religion—Heaven's greatest boon to man—was destined, by the clear announcements of prophecy, to fill the world; and it was deemed the duty of the Church to extend these triumphs in all possible ways. The importance of the end to be attained, it was thought, would sanctify even the instrumentality of violence and blood. Wealth and honors were among the earthly rewards promised to the faithful.

Allowances must be made for the darkness of the age. It is by very slow and painful steps that the human mind has attained to even its present unsteady position in regard to civil and religious rights.

The Governor of Cuba, Velasquez, looked earnestly for a man to head this important enterprise. He found just the man for the occasion in Hernando Cortez—a fearless, energetic Spanish adventurer, then residing upon the island of Cuba. His early life will be found in the next chapter.

CHAPTER II.
EARLY LIFE OF CORTEZ.

IN the interior of Spain, in the midst of the sombre mountains whose confluent streams compose the waters of the Guadiana, there reposes the little village or hamlet of Medellin. A more secluded spot it would be difficult to find. Three hundred and seventy years ago, in the year 1485, Hernando Cortez was born in this place. His ancestors had enjoyed wealth and rank. The family was now poor, but proud of the Castilian blood which flowed in their veins. The father of Hernando was a captain in the army—a man of honorable character. Of his mother but little is known.

Not much has been transmitted to our day respecting the childhood of this extraordinary man. It is reported that he early developed a passion for wild adventure; that he was idle and wayward; frank, fearless, and generous; that he loved to explore the streams and to climb the cliffs of his mountainous home, and that he ever appeared reckless of danger. He was popular with his companions, for warm-heartedness and magnanimity were prominent in his character.

His father, though struggling with poverty, cherished ambitious views for his son, and sent him to the celebrated university of Salamanca for an education. He wished Hernando to avoid the perils and temptations of the camp, and to enter the honorable profession of the law. Hernando reluctantly obeyed the wishes of his father, and went to the university. But he scorned restraint. He despised all the employments of industry, and study was his especial abhorrence. Two years were worse than wasted in the university. Young Cortez was both indolent and dissipated. In all the feats of mischief he was the ringleader, and his books were entirely neglected. He received many censures, and was on the point of being expelled, when his disappointed father withdrew the wayward boy from the halls of the university, and took him home.

Hernando was now sixteen years of age. There was nothing for him to do in the seclusion of his native village but to indulge in idleness. This he did with great diligence. He rode horses; he hunted and fished; he learned the art of the swordsman and played the soldier. Hot blood glowed in his veins, and he became genteelly dissolute; his pride would never allow him to stoop to vulgarity. The father was grief-stricken by the misconduct of his son, and at last consented to gratify the passion which inspired him to become a soldier.

At seventeen years of age the martial boy enlisted in an expedition, under Gonsalvo de Cordova, to assist the Italians against the French. Young Cortez, to his bitter disappointment, just as the expedition started, was taken seriously sick, and was obliged to be left behind. Soon after this, one of his relatives was appointed, by the Spanish crown, governor of St. Domingo, now called Hayti, but then called Hispaniola, or Little Spain. This opening to scenes and adventures in the New World was attractive to the young cavalier in the highest possible degree. It was, indeed, an enterprise which might worthily arouse the enthusiasm of any mind. A large fleet was equipped to convey nearly three thousand settlers to found a colony beneath the sunny skies and under the orange groves of the tropics. Life there seemed the elysium of the indolent man. Young Cortez now rejoiced heartily over his previous disappointment. His whole soul was engrossed in the contemplation of the wild and romantic adventures in which he expected to luxuriate. It is not to be supposed that a lad of such a temperament should, at the age of seventeen, be a stranger to the passion of love. There was a young lady in his native village for whom he had formed a strong youthful attachment. He resolved, with his accustomed ardor and recklessness, to secure an interview with his lady-love, where parting words and pledges should not be witnessed by prudent relatives.

One dark night, just before the squadron sailed, the ardent lover climbed a mouldering wall to reach the window of the young lady's chamber. In the obscurity he slipped and fell, and some heavy stones from the crumbling wall fell upon him. He was conveyed to his bed, severely wounded and helpless. The fleet sailed, and the young man, almost insane with disappointment and chagrin, was left upon his bed of pain.

At length he recovered. His father secured for him a passage to join the colonists in another ship. He, with exultation, left Medellin, hastened to the sea-shore, where he embarked.

and after an unusually adventurous and perilous voyage, he gazed with delight upon the tropical vegetation and the new scenes of life of Hispaniola. It was the year 1504. Cortez was then nineteen years of age.

The young adventurer, immediately upon landing, proceeded to the house of his relative, Governor Ovando. The governor happened to be absent, but his secretary received the young man very cordially.

"I have no doubt," said he to Hernando, "that you will receive a liberal grant of land to cultivate."

"I come to get gold," Hernando replied, haughtily, "not to till the soil like a peasant."

Ovando, on his return, took his young relative under his patronage, and assigned to him posts of profit and honor. Still Cortez was very restless. His impatient spirit wearied of the routine of daily duty, and his imagination was ever busy in the domain of wild adventure.

Two Spaniards upon the island of Hispaniola about this time planned an expedition for exploring the main land, to make discoveries and to select spots for future settlements. Cortez eagerly joined the enterprise, but again was he doomed to disappointment. Just before the vessels sailed he was seized by a fever, and laid prostrate upon his bed. Probably his life was thus saved. Nearly all who embarked on this enterprise perished by storm, disease, and the poisoned arrows of the natives.

Seven years passed away, during which Cortez led an idle and voluptuous life, ever ready for any daring adventure which might offer, and miserably attempting to beguile the weariness of provincial life with guilty amours. He accepted a plantation from the governor, which was cultivated by slaves. His purse was thus ever well filled. Not unfrequently he became involved in duels, and he bore upon his body until death many scars received in these encounters. Military expeditions were not unfrequently sent out to quell the insurrections to which the natives of the island were goaded by the injustice and the cruelty of the Spaniards.

Cortez was always an eager volunteer for such service. His courage and imperturbable self-possession made him an invaluable co-operator in every enterprise of danger. He thus became acquainted with all the artifices of Indian warfare, and inured himself to the toil and privations of forest life.

In the year 1492 the magnificent island of

Cuba, but a few leagues from Hispaniola, had been discovered by Columbus. As he approached the land, the grandeur of the mountains, the wide sweep of the valleys, the stately forests, the noble rivers, the bold promontories and headlands, melting away in the blue of the hazy distance, impressed him with unbounded admiration. As he sailed up one of the beautiful rivers of crystal clearness, fringed with flowers, and aromatic shrubs, and tropical fruits, while the overhanging trees were vocal with the melody of birds of every variety of song and plumage, enraptured he exclaimed,

"Cuba! It is the most beautiful island that eyes ever beheld. It is an elysium. One could live there forever."

The natives of the favored land were amiable and friendly. The Spaniards did not for several years encroach upon their rights, and no Spanish colony was established upon their enchanting shores. It was now the year 1511. Nineteen years had elapsed since the discovery of the island. Ovando had been recalled, and Diego Columbus, the son of Christopher, had been appointed, in his stead, governor of Hispaniola. He took the title of Viceroy, and assumed all the splendors of royalty. Diego Columbus devoutly decided that it was manifest destiny that Cuba should belong to Spain. He organized a *filibustering* expedition to wrest from the natives their beautiful island. The command of the expedition was intrusted to Don Velasquez, a bold adventurer, of much notoriety, from Spain, who had been residing for many years at Hispaniola, and who had been lieutenant under Governor Ovando. A foray of this kind would, of course, excite the patriotic zeal of every vagabond. Cortez was one of the first to hasten to the standard of Velasquez. The natives of the island, unarmed and voluptuous, made hardly the shadow of resistance, and three hundred Spanish adventurers, with but a slight struggle, took possession of this magnificent domain. The reputation and ability of Cortez gave him a prominent position in this adventure.

One brave and patriotic Indian chief, who had fled from the outrages perpetrated at Hispaniola, urged the Cubans to repel the invaders. Though unable to rouse in a mass the peace-loving islanders, he gathered a small band around him, and valiantly contended to resist the landing. His efforts were quite unavailing. Gunpowder soon triumphed. The Indians were speedily put to flight, and the chieftain Hatuey was taken prisoner.

Velasquez ignobly and cruelly condemned the heroic patriot to be burned alive; but religiously the fanatic invader wished, though he burned the body, to save the soul. A priest was appointed to labor for the conversion of the victim.

"If you will embrace our religion," said the priest, "as soon as the fire has consumed your body, you will enter heaven, and be happy there forever."

"Are there Spaniards," inquired Hatuey, "in that happy place of which you speak?"

"Yes," replied the priest; "such as are holy."

"Then I will not go there!" Hatuey energetically rejoined. "I will never go to a place where I shall meet one of that cruel people."

The poor Indian was burned to ashes. The natives gazed upon the spectacle with horror. They were appalled, and ventured to make no farther resistance to their terrible conquerors.

Such is Spain's title-deed to the island of Cuba. God has not smiled upon regions thus infamously won. May the United States take warning that all her possessions may be honorably acquired. "God helps," says blind unbelief, "the heavy battalions;" but experience has fully proved that "the race is not always to the swift, nor the battle to the strong."

One or two colonies were soon established upon the conquered island. They grew very rapidly. Velasquez was appointed governor; Cortez was his secretary.

Many families were enticed from Spain by the charms of this most beautiful of the isles of the ocean. A gentleman came from old Castile with four beautiful daughters. Velasquez became attached to one; Cortez trifled grievously with the affections of another. The governor reproached him for his infamous conduct. The proud spirit of Cortez could not brook reproof, and he entered into a conspiracy to proffer complaints against the governor, and to secure his removal. It was a bold and a perilous undertaking.

Cortez prepared to embark in an open boat, and push out fearlessly but secretly into the open sea, to make a voyage of nearly sixty miles to Hispaniola. There he was to enter his complaints to Diego Columbus. The conspiracy was detected upon the eve of its execution. Cortez was arrested, manacled, thrown into prison, and was, after trial, sentenced to death for treason. He, however, succeeded in breaking his fetters, forced open his prison window, and dropped himself down, in the darkness of the night, from the second story, and escaped to the sanctuary of a neighboring church. Such a sanctuary, in that day, could not be violated.

A guard was secreted to watch him. He remained in the church for several days. But at length impatience triumphed over prudence, and, as he attempted one night to escape, he was again arrested, more strongly chained, and was placed on board a ship to be sent to Hispaniola for execution.

The code of Spanish law was in that day a bloody one. Spanish governors were almost unlimited despots. Cortez was not willing to go to Hispaniola with the cord of a convicted traitor about his neck. With extraordinary fortitude, he drew his feet, mangling them sadly, through the irons which shackled them. Creeping cautiously upon deck, he let himself down softly into the water, swam to the shore, and, half dead with pain and exhaustion, attained again the sanctuary of the church.

He now consented to marry the young lady with whose affections and reputation he had so cruelly trifled. The family, of course, espoused his cause. The governor, who was the lover of her sister, regarded this as the *amende honorable*, and again received the hot-blooded cavalier to his confidence. Thus this black and threatening cloud suddenly disappeared, and sunshine and calm succeeded the storm. Cortez returned to his estates with his bride a wiser, and perhaps a better man, from the severe discipline through which he had passed. Catalina Suarez, whom he married, was an amiable and beautiful lady of very estimable character. She eventually quite won the love of her wayward and fickle husband.

"I lived as happily with her," said the haughty Castilian, "as if she had been the daughter of a duchess."

Velasquez, like every other Spanish governor at that time, was ambitious of extending his dominions. In the year 1517, a number of restless spirits, under his patronage, resolved to sail upon a voyage of discovery and conquest.

Three vessels were fitted out for this adventure. One hundred and ten men embarked in the enterprise, under the command of Francisco Hernandez, of Cordova. Velasquez directed them to land upon some neighboring islands, and seize a number of inhabitants, and make slaves of them, to pay the cost of the expedition. "But when the proposal," says one of the party, "was made known to the soldiers, we to a man refused it, saying that it was not just, nor did God or the king permit that free men should be made slaves. That our expedition," the same writer continues, "might be conducted on proper principles, we persuaded a clergyman to accompany us." In fervent prayer, commending themselves to God and the Virgin, they unfurled their sails, and steered resolutely toward the setting sun. They discovered the island of Cozumel and the vast promontory of Yucatan.* The expedition, however, encountered many disasters. The natives assailed them fiercely. At length the shattered ships returned, having lost seventy men, and bringing with them quite a number bleeding and dying. Cordova died of his wounds ten days after arriving at Havana.

The tidings, however, of the magnificent discovery, and the fabulous report that the country was rich in gold, incited Velasquez to fit

* *Yuca* is the Indian name of the plant used for bread. The heap of earth in which it is planted is called *tule*. The two words repeated together made Yucatul, or Yucatan as it was expressed by the Spaniards.—*Bernal Diaz*, p. 10.

out a second expedition of four ships, under the command of Juan de Grijalva. Two hundred and forty adventurers embarked in the enterprise. On the 5th day of April, 1518, after having devoutly partaken of the sacrament of the Lord's Supper, the anchors were lifted, and the little squadron sailed from the port of Matanzas. Eight days brought them to Cozumel. They then passed over to the continent, and coasted along the shore for many leagues to the north and west. They made frequent attempts to land and open intercourse with the natives, but they were invariaby attacked with the utmost determination. Though the Spaniards were generally victorious in these conflicts, they lost several men, and very many were sorely wounded. At length they arrived upon the coast of Mexico, and landed at the point now called St. Juan de Ulua. Here they were kindly received by the natives, and acquired considerable gold in exchange for glass beads. They also obtained vague information of the great monarch Montezuma, and of the extent and power of his realms. Greatly elated with this success, Grijalva sent one of his vessels back to Cuba with specimens of the gold, and with most glowing accounts of the grandeur, wealth, and power of the newly-discovered empire of Mexico. To their extreme delight, the voyagers found that the natives had hatchets apparently of solid burnished gold. The excitement was intense on board the ships. Six hundred of these hatchets were eagerly bought. At length the expedition returned to Cuba. The six hundred golden hatchets were triumphantly displayed, when, to the unutterable chagrin of their possessors, they proved to be but copper. The disappointed adventurers were overwhelmed with ridicule. "There was much laughter," says Diaz, who accompanied the expedition, "when the six hundred hatchets were produced and assayed."

The tidings of the discovery of Mexico spread, however, like wildfire over the island of Cuba. Every bosom which could be moved by avarice or by the love of adventure was intensely excited. Velasquez promptly dispatched the welcome intelligence to Spain, and immediately commenced fitting out another expedition upon a scale of grandeur hitherto unattempted. No one heard these tidings with such a thrill of emotion as Hernando Cortez. Though enjoying a rich estate, his extravagance had involved him in debt and distress. To retrieve his ruined fortunes, and to gratify his insatiable love of adventure, he resolved to leave no efforts untried to secure for himself the command of the expedition.

He bribed some of the powerful friends of the governor to advocate his cause, promising them a rich share of the booty which he hoped to obtain. He also offered to contribute largely of his own wealth to fit out the naval armament.

It was manifest to all that there could not be a man better adapted to fill such a post than Hernando Cortez. The governor was well instructed in his energy, capacity, and courage. But he feared these traits of character. He wished for a man who would act as his agent, who would be submissive to his authority, and who would transfer the glory of successful achievement to his name. But Cortez was a man to lead, not to be led. The governor hesitated. At last he yielded to the powerful considerations which were pressed upon him, and publicly announced Cortez as captain general of the armada.

As soon as Cortez received this commission, all the glowing enthusiasm and tremendous energy of his nature were roused and concentrated upon this one magnificent object. His whole character seemed suddenly to experience a total change. He became serious, earnest, thoughtful. Mighty destinies were in his hands. Deeds were to be accomplished at which the world was to marvel. Strange as it may seem, for the heart of man is an inexplicable enigma, religion, perhaps we should say religious fanaticism, mingled the elements of her mystic power in the motives which inspired the soul of this extraordinary man. He was to march the apostle of Christianity to overthrow the idols in the halls of Montezuma, and there to rear the cross of Christ. It was his heavenly mission to convert the benighted Indians to the religion of Jesus. With the energies of fire and sword, misery and blood, horses rushing to the charge and death-dealing artillery, he was to lead back the wandering victims of darkness and sin to those paths of piety which guide to heaven.

Such was Hernando Cortez. Let Philosophy explain the enigma as she may, no intelligent man will venture the assertion that Cortez was a hypocrite. He was a frank, fearless, deluded enthusiast.

Governor Velasquez soon became alarmed in view of the independent energy with which Cortez pressed forward the enterprise. It was quite evident that the bold adventurer would regard no instructions, and that, having acquired wealth and fame, he would, with his commanding genius, become a formidable rival. Velasquez therefore determined, before it should be too late, to deprive Cortez of the command. But it was already too late. The energetic captain received from a friend an intimation of his peril. With the decision which marked his character, he that very night, though the vessels were not prepared for sea, and the complement of men was not yet mustered, resolved secretly to weigh anchor.

The moment the sun went down he called upon his officers and informed them of his purpose. Every man was instantly and silently in motion. At midnight the little squadron, with all on board, dropped down the bay. Intelligence was promptly conveyed to the governor of this sudden and unexpected departure. Mounting his horse, he galloped to a point of the shore which commanded a view of the fleet at anchor in the roadstead. Cortez, from the deck of his ship, saw the governor upon the beach surrounded by his retinue. He entered a boat and was rowed near to the shore. The governor reproached Cortez bitterly for his conduct.

"Pardon me," said the captain, courteously; "time presses, and there are some things which should be done before they are even thought of."

Then, with Castilian grace, waving an adieu to the governor, he returned to his ship. The anchors were immediately raised, the sails spread, and the little fleet, the renown of whose extraordinary achievements was to fill the world, was wafted from the harbor of St. Jago, and soon disappeared in the distant horizon of the sea.

St. Jago was then the capital of Cuba. Cortez directed his course to Mocaca, about thirty miles distant. Hastily collecting such additional stores as the place would afford, he again weighed anchor and proceeded to Trinidad. This was an important town on the southern shore of the island. Here he landed, raised his banner, and, with alluring promises, invited volunteers to join the expedition. He marshaled and drilled his men, collected military supplies, and, more than all, by the charms of his daily intercourse secured the enthusiastic devotion of his followers.

His men were armed with cross-bows and

CORTEZ TAKING LEAVE OF THE GOVERNOR.

muskets, and he had several small cannon. Jackets, thickly wadded with cotton, were provided as coats of mail for the soldiers, which were a great protection against the missiles of the natives. Neither arrow nor javelin could pierce them. A black velvet banner, embroidered with gold, and emblazoned with a cross, bore the characteristic device,

"Let us follow the cross. Under this sign, with faith, we conquer."

Beneath such a standard did these stern men march upon an expedition of wanton aggression, crime, and woe.

A trading vessel appeared off the coast, laden with provisions and valuable merchandise. It was a providential gift of exactly that which the adventurers needed. Cortez, with gratitude to God, seized both ship and cargo, and by his peculiar powers of moral suasion induced the captain and most of the crew to enlist in his service. Another ship made its appearance; it was a renewed token of God's kindness to his servants; it was received with alacrity. Whatever remonstrances the owners might raise were drowned in thanksgivings and praises. Every movement of the expedition was inspired by the fanatical spirit of the Crusades.

Cortez now, with his force much strengthened, sailed around the western point of the island to Havana. With renewed diligence, he here resumed his labor of beating up recruits and of augmenting his stores. Governor Velasquez, informed of his arrival at this port, dispatched orders to Pedro Barba, commander at Havana, to arrest Cortez and seize the fleet. But it was much easier to issue this order than to execute it. Cortez was now too strong to be apprehended by any force which Barba had at his command. Cortez received from a friend an intimation of the order for his arrest which had been received from the governor.

He assembled his bold followers around him; made a rousing speech, full of eloquence and of the peculiar piety then in vogue; painted in glowing colors the wealth and the renown opening before them in the vast realms of Mexico; and then portrayed, with biting sarcasm, the jealousy and the meanness of Velasquez, who wished to deprive him of the command of the enterprise.

The speech was convincing. His tumultuary followers threw up their hats and filled the air with acclamations. They declared that they would acknowledge Cortez, and Cortez only,

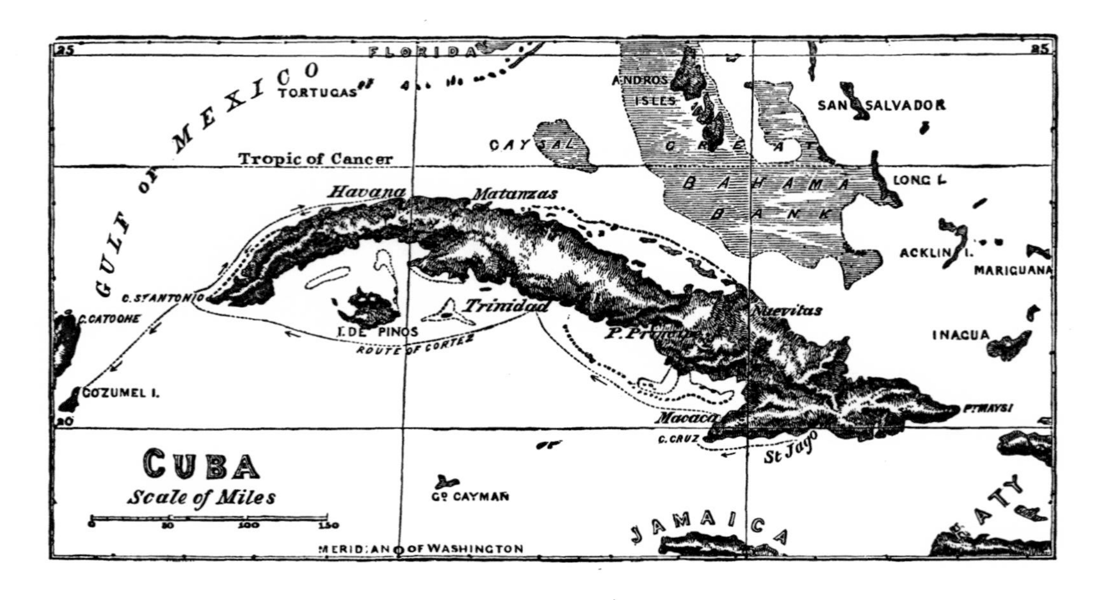
FLORIDA
GULF OF MEXICO
TORTUGAS
Tropic of Cancer
CAY SAL
ANDROS ISLES
GREAT BAHAMA BANK
SAN SALVADOR
LONG I.
ACKLIN I.
MARIGUANA
INAGUA
Havana
Matanzas
Nuevitas
Trinidad
P. Principe
Macaca
C. CRUZ
St Jago
P.T MAYSI
C. S.T ANTONIO
C. CATOCHE
COZUMEL I.
I. DE PINOS
ROUTE OF CORTEZ
G.D CAYMAN
JAMAICA
CUBA
Scale of Miles
0
50
100
150
MERIDIAN OF WASHINGTON
25
20
25

as their leader; that they would follow him wherever he might guide; that they would defend him with their lives, and that they would wreak unsparing vengeance upon any enemies who should attempt to molest him in his glorious career. This was the efficient reply which Cortez made to the order for his arrest.

The reply was not lost upon Barba. He perceived that it would be folly to attempt to execute the command of the governor. He wrote to him accordingly, stating the impracticability of the attempt. In fact, Barba had no disposition to arrest Cortez. He had become strongly attached to the bold and earnest captain. Cortez himself also wrote a very courteous letter to the governor, with studied politeness informing him that, with the blessing of God, he should sail the next day, and assuring the governor of eternal devotion to his interest. As there was some danger that Velasquez might send from St. Jago a force sufficiently strong to cause some embarrassment, the little squadron the next morning weighed anchor and proceeded to Cape Antonio, an appointed place of rendezvous on the extreme western termination of the island.

Here Cortez completed his preparations and

collected all the force he desired. He had now eleven vessels. The largest was of but one hundred tons. Three were of but seventy tons, and the rest were open barks. His whole force consisted of one hundred and ten seamen, five hundred and fifty-three soldiers, two hundred Indians, and a few Indian women for menial service. His regular soldiers consisted of sixteen horsemen, thirty musketeers, and thirty-two cross-bowmen. He had also, as the most formidable part of his armament, fourteen pieces of artillery, with an ample supply of ammunition. All the soldiers, excepting the musketeers and the bowmen, were armed simply with swords and spears. Sixteen horses formed also an exceedingly important part of the physical force of the army. This noble animal had never yet been seen on the continent of America. With great difficulty, a few had been transported across the ocean from Spain. With such a force this enthusiastic adventurer undertook the subjugation of a nation of many millions.

Cortez was now thirty-three years of age. He was a handsome, well-formed man, of medium stature, of pale, intellectual features, with a piercing, dark eye, and frank and winning manners. He was temperate, indifferent respecting all personal comforts, and reckless of hardship and peril. He fully appreciated the influence of dress, and ever appeared in the rich garb of a Spanish gentleman. He was courtly yet frank in his manners, and possessed a peculiar power of attracting to his person all who approached him.

On the eve of his departure from Cape Antonio, he again assembled his followers around him, and thus harangued them:

"The enterprise in which you are engaged will fill the world with your renown. I am leading you to countries more vast and opulent than European eyes have ever yet beheld. It is a glorious prize which I present to you. But this prize can only be won by hardship and toil. Great deeds are only achieved by great exertions. Glory is never the reward of sloth. I have labored hard and staked my all on this undertaking, for I love that renown which is the noblest recompense of man.

"Do you covet riches more? Be true to me, and I will make you masters of wealth of which you have never dreamed. You are few in numbers, but be strong in resolution, and doubt not that the Almighty, who has never deserted the

Spaniard in his contest with the infidel, will shield you, though encompassed by enemies. Your cause is just. You are to fight under the banner of the cross. Onward, then, with alacrity. Gloriously terminate the work so auspiciously begun."

This speech was received with tumultuous cheers. Mass was then celebrated by the ecclesiastics who accompanied the fleet, and with many religious ceremonies the squadron was placed under the protection of St. Peter. The anchors were raised, the sails were spread, and a favoring breeze pressed them rapidly over the waves toward the setting sun. It was the 18th of February, 1519.

CHAPTER III.

THE VOYAGE TO MEXICO.

LIGHT and variable winds retarded the progress of the squadron as it was headed in a southwesterly direction toward the shores of Yucatan. A terrible tempest succeeded, and the ships were driven wildly before the storm. But after the lapse of about a week, as the storm abated, they were cheered by the sight of land. The mountains of the island of Cozumel rose towering before them. This large island is separated from the main land of Yucatan by a channel of from twelve to thirty miles in width.

When the natives saw the ships approaching, they fled from the shores in terror. Such a fleet must have, indeed, presented to the artless inhabitants an appalling spectacle. The squadron cast anchor in a spacious bay, and those who first arrived were the first to land. The captain of one of the vessels, with some of his crew, entered one of the native temples, and, seeing the idol decorated with gold, seized the treasure promptly as lawful prize, and also captured two or three of the natives. Cortez was indignant at conduct so rash and impolitic. He severely rebuked the over-zealous captain, ordered the ornaments to be replaced, and liberated the captives and loaded them with presents. He thus appeased the fears of the natives, and induced them to return to their dwellings. They soon became quite reconciled to the strangers, and opened with them a lucrative traffic. The island was not very fertile, and was thinly inhabited; but the natives had large and comfortable houses, built of stone cemented with mortar. There were several spacious temples, with lofty towers, constructed of the same durable materials. The adventurers were also exceedingly surprised to find in the court-yard of one of the temples an idol in the form of a massive stone cross. It was erected in honor of the god of rain. It is, indeed, a curious question, and one which probably will never be answered, how the natives of this new world obtained those apparently shadowy ideas of Christianity. They certainly performed the rite of baptism. The cross was one of their idols. They also believed in original sin, which was to be in some way removed by sprinkling an infant with water.

Cortez remained upon this island about a fortnight. During this time all his energies were engrossed in accomplishing the great object of his mission. He sent two vessels to the main land to make inquiries about some Spaniards, who, it was reported, had been shipwrecked upon the coast, and were still lingering in captivity. The captain in command of this expedition was instructed to return within eight days. Several parties were also sent in various directions to explore the island thoroughly and ascertain its resources.

But one of the most important objects, in the estimation of Cortez, to be accomplished, was the conversion of the natives to the Catholic religion. He had with him several ecclesiastics —men whose sincerity no candid man can doubt. The Indians were assembled, and urged, through an interpreter, to abandon their idols and turn to the living God. The simple natives understood but little of the harangue, except the injunction to destroy their idols. At this suggestion they were horror-stricken. They assured Cortez that were they to harm or insult their gods, destruction in every awful form would immediately overwhelm them.

The bold warrior wielded bold arguments.

His logic was truly military. With his mailed cavaliers he made a prompt onslaught upon the idols, hewed them down, smashed them to pieces, and tumbled the dishonored and mutilated fragments into the streets. He then constructed a Christian altar, reared a cross and an image of the holy Virgin and the holy child, and mass, with all its pomp of robes, and chants, and incense, was for the first time performed in the temples of Yucatan.

The natives were at first overwhelmed with grief and terror as they gazed upon their prostrate deities. But no earthquake shook the island; no lightning sped its angry bolt; no thunder broke down the skies. The sun still shone tranquilly, and ocean, earth, and sky smiled untroubled. The natives ceased to fear gods who could not protect themselves, and without farther argument consented to exchange their ungainly idols for the far prettier idols of the strangers. The heart of Cortez throbbed with enthusiasm and pride as he contemplated his great and glorious achievement—an achievement, in his view, unparalleled by the miracles of Peter or of Paul. In one short fortnight he had converted these islanders from the service of Satan, and had won them to that faith which would

THE FIRST MASS IN THE TEMPLES OF YUCATAN

secure their eternal salvation. The fanatic sincerity with which this deed was accomplished does not redeem it from the sublimity of absurdity. Faith, said these mailed theologians, saves the soul; and these pagans have now turned from their idols to the living God. It is true that man is saved by faith, but it is that faith which *works by love.*

In the mean time the parties returned from the exploration of the island, and Orday brought back his two ships from the main land. He was unsuccessful in his attempts to find the shipwrecked Spaniards. Cortez had now been at Cozumel a fortnight. As he was on the point of taking his departure, a frail canoe was seen crossing the strait, with three men in it, apparently Indians, and entirely naked. As soon as the canoe landed, one of the men ran frantically to the Spaniards and informed them that he was a Christian and a countryman. His name was Aguilar.

Seven years ago, the vessel in which he was sailing from Darien to Hispaniola foundered in a gale. The ship's company, twenty in number, took to the boats. For thirteen days they were driven about at the mercy of the winds and currents. Seven perished miserably from hunger and thirst. The rest reached the barbarian shores of Yucatan. The natives seized them as captives, guarded them carefully, but fed them abundantly with the choicest food, and inflicted upon them no sufferings, and required of them no toil. Their treatment was an enigma which was soon dreadfully explained.

One day four of these captives who were in the best condition were selected, sacrificed upon the bloody altars of the idols, and their cooked flesh served up for a cannibal repast. The howlings of the savages over the midnight orgies of this horrible entertainment fell dismally upon the ears of the miserable survivors. In their despair they succeeded in escaping, and fled to the mountain forests. Here they wandered for a time in the endurance of awful sufferings. At length they were again taken captive by the cacique or chief of another province. He spared their lives, but made them menial slaves. Their masters were merciless and exacting in the extreme. Under this rigorous treatment all died but two—Aguilar, a priest, and Guerrero, a sailor. The sailor, having no scruples of any kind, and being ready to conform himself to all customs, gradually acquired the good will of the savages. He obtained renown as a warrior; identified himself entirely with the natives; tattooed his face; slit his ears, his lips, and his nose, for those dangling ornaments which ever accompany a barbarian taste, and took to him a native wife.

Aguilar, however, was a man of more cultivation and refinement. He cherished his self-respect, and, resisting all enticements to marry an Indian maiden, was true to the vows of celibacy which his priestly profession imposed. Curious stories are related of the temptations to which the natives exposed him. Weary years lingered along, presenting no opportunity for escape. Cortez at last arrived at Cozumel. Some Indians carried the tidings into the interior. Aguilar received this intelligence with transport, and yet with trembling. He, however, succeeded in reaching the coast, accompanied by two friendly natives. He found upon the beach a stranded canoe, half buried in the sand. Embarking in this with his two companions, they paddled themselves across the strait, at that place twelve miles wide, to the island. The frail boat was seen by the party of Cortez upon the surface of the sea. As soon as Aguilar landed he dropped upon his knees, and with streaming eyes gave thanks to God for his escape.

His companion in captivity refused to accompany him. "Brother Aguilar," said he, after a moment's thought, "I am married. I have three sons, and am a cacique and captain in the wars. My face is tattooed and my ears bored. What would the Spaniards think of me should I now go among them?" All Aguilar's entreaties for him to leave were unavailing.

Aguilar appears to have been truly a good man. As he had acquired a perfect acquaintance with the language of the natives, and with their manners and customs, Cortez received him as a heaven-sent acquisition to his enterprise.

On the 4th of March the squadron again set sail, and, crossing the narrow strait, approached the shores of the continent. Sailing directly north some hundred miles, hugging the coast of Yucatan, Cortez doubled Cape Catoche, and turning his prow to the west, boldly pressed forward into those unknown waters which seemed to extend interminably before him. The shores were densely covered with the luxuriant foliage of the tropics, and in many a bay and on many a headland could be discerned the thronged dwellings of the natives.

After sailing west about two hundred miles, they found the coast again turning abruptly to the south. Following the line of the land some three hundred miles farther, they came to the broad mouth of the River Tabasco, which Grijalva had entered, and which Cortez was seeking. A sand-bar at the mouth of the river prevented the heavily-loaded vessels from passing. Cortez, therefore, cast anchor, and taking a strong and well-armed party in the boats, ascended the shallow stream.

A forest of majestic trees, with underwood dense and impervious, lined the banks. The naked forms of the natives were seen gliding among the foliage, following, in rapidly-accumulating numbers, the advance of the boats, and evincing, by tone and gesture, any thing but a friendly spirit. At last, arriving at an opening in the forest, where a smooth and grassy meadow extended with gradual ascent from the stream, the boats drew near the shore, and Cortez, through his interpreter Aguilar, asked permission to land, avowing his friendly intentions. The prompt answer was the clash of weapons and shouts of defiance.

Upon this Cortez decided to postpone a forcible landing until the morning, and retired to a small island in the river which was uninhabited. He here encamped for the night, establishing a vigilant line of sentinels to guard against surprise.

In the early dawn of the next morning the party were assembled for prayers and for the celebration of mass. They then, with new zeal and courage, entered their boats, and ascended the glassy, forest-fringed stream, upon which the morning sun shone brightly. Bird-songs filled the air, and hardly a breath of wind moved the leaves, glittering in the brilliant sunlight, as these bronzed men of iron sinews moved sternly on to the demoniac deeds of war. The natives, in preparation for the conflict, had been all the night rallying their forces. The shore was lined with their war-canoes, and the banks were covered with Indian troops drawn up in martial array. Gorgeous plumes decorated their persons, and the rays of the sun were reflected from their polished weapons. As soon as the Spanish boats appeared, the vast army of the natives raised shouts of defiance, and the ear was almost deafened with the clangor of their trumpets and drums.

The battle soon commenced. The sky was almost darkened by the shower of arrows thrown by those upon the land. The warriors in the canoes fought fiercely with their javelins. The conflict was bloody, but short. Native valor could avail but little against European discipline and art. The spears, stones, and arrows of the natives fell almost harmless upon the helmets and shields of the Spaniards; but the bullets from the guns of the invaders swept like hail-stones through the crowded ranks of the natives, unimpeded by their frail weapons of defense. Cortez himself headed a charge which broke resistlessly into the hostile ranks. Appalled by the terrific thunder and lightning of the musketry, the Indians soon scattered and fled, leaving the ground covered with their slain.

Cortez now reviewed his troops in triumph upon the shore. He found that fourteen were wounded, but none slain. To attend to the wounded and to rest his exhausted men, he again encamped. The bloodstained banner of the cross, which they had so signally dishonored, floated proudly over their intrenchments. Prayers were offered and mass celebrated in honor of the victory achieved by Christian arms against idolaters. The next morning the Spaniards marched unresisted to Tabasco, the capital of the province, a large town upon the river.

but a few miles above the place where the invaders had effected a landing. The inhabitants, men, women, and children, fled from the place in dismay.

Cortez took possession of the town in the name of the King of Spain. But the whole surrounding region was now aroused. The natives, in numbers which could not be counted, gathered in the vicinity of Tabasco, and organized their forces anew, to repel, if possible, the terrible foe. They were assembled on the great plain of Ceutla. Cortez had anticipated this, and was also gathering his strength for a decisive battle. He sent to the ships for six pieces of cannon, his whole cavalry of sixteen horses, and every available man. A few only were left to guard the vessels. This powerful re-enforcement soon arrived. Thus strengthened, his whole army was called together to celebrate the solemnities of mass, and to implore the blessing of God in extending the triumphs of the cross over the kingdom of Satan. Thus they marched forth, with powder, and ball, and neighing steeds, to the merciless slaughter of those brave men who were fighting for their country and their homes.

The Spaniards now advanced to meet their

foes. It was a lovely morning, the 25th of March. The natives, in point of civilization, raised far above the condition of savages, had large fields in a high state of cultivation, waving with the rich vegetation of the tropics. After a march of three or four miles through a country cultivated like a garden, they arrived at the ground occupied by the native army. The lines of their encampments were so extended and yet so crowded that the Spaniards estimated their numbers at over forty thousand. To meet them in the strife Cortez had but six hundred men. But his terrible engines of destruction made his force more powerful than theirs. The natives were ready for the battle. They greeted their assailants with a war-whoop, which rose in thunder tones over the plain, and showered upon them volleys of arrows, sling-stones, and javelins. At this first discharge, seventy Spaniards were wounded and one was slain. The conflict soon raged with all imaginable horrors. The natives fought with the courage of desperation. They seemed even regardless of the death-dealing muskets. And when the terrible cannon, with its awful roar, opened huge gaps in their ranks, manfully they closed up, and with new vigor pressed the onset. The odds were so fearful that for some time it seemed quite doubtful on which side victory would rest.

Cortez, heading his cavalry, swept around the plain, and, by a circuitous route, came unperceived upon the rear of the tumultuous foe. The sixteen horsemen, clad in steel, urging their horses to their utmost speed, with loud shouts and sabres gleaming in the air, plunged into the midst of the throng. Their keen-edged swords fell on the right hand and on the left upon the almost naked bodies of the natives. At the same moment, the energies of musketry and artillery were plied with murderous carnage.

The natives had never seen a horse before. They thought the rider and the steed one animal. As these terrific monsters, half human, half beast, came bounding into their midst, cutting down and trampling beneath iron hoofs all who stood in the way, while at the same time the appalling roar of the cannonade seemed to shake the very hills, the scene became too awful for mortal courage to endure. The whole mighty mass, in uncontrollable dismay, fled from the presence of foes of such demoniac aspect and energy. The slaughter of these poor

FIRST CAVALRY CHARGE HEADED BY CO[illegible]

Indians was so awful that some of the Spaniards extravagantly estimated the number left dead upon the field at thirty thousand. Though many of the Spaniards were wounded, but two were killed.

Cortez immediately assembled his army under a grove upon the field of battle to give thanks to God for the victory. The pomp and pageantry of war gave place to the pomp and pageantry of the Church. Canonical robes and banners fluttered in the breeze, processions marched, the smoke of incense floated in the air, and mass, with all its imposing solemnities, was celebrated in the midst of prayers and thanksgivings.

"Then," says Diaz, "after dressing our wounds with the fat of Indians whom we found dead thereabout, and having placed good guards round our post, we ate our supper and went to our repose."

Under the placable influence of these devotions, the conqueror sent word to the vanquished that he would now *forgive them* if they would submit unconditionally to his authority. But he declared that if they refused this, he would ride over the land, and put every thing in it, man, woman, and child, to the sword.

The spirit of resistance was utterly crushed. The natives immediately sent a delegation to him laden with presents. To impress these embassadors still more deeply with a sense of his power, he exhibited before them the martial evolutions of his cavalry, and showed them the effects of his artillery as the balls were sped crashing through the trees of the forest. The natives were now effectually conquered, and looked upon the Spaniards as beings of supernatural powers, wielding the terrors of thunder and lightning, and whom no mortal energies could resist.

They had become as little children. This Cortez thought a very suitable frame of mind to secure their conversion. He recommended that they should cast down their idols, and accept instead the gods of papal Rome. The recommendation of Cortez was potent over the now pliant natives. They made no opposition while the soldiers, whose hands were hardly yet washed of the blood of their relatives, hewed down their images. With very imposing ceremonies, the religion of the conquerors was instituted in the temples of Yucatan, and, in honor of the Virgin Mary, the name of Tabasco was changed into St. Mary of Victory.

In all this tremendous crime there was apparently no hypocrisy. Human motives will seldom bear rigid scrutiny. Man's best deeds are tainted. Cortez was very sincere in his desire to overthrow the abominable system of idolatry prevailing among the natives. He perhaps truly thought that these violent measures were necessary to accomplish this object, and that Christianity, thus introduced, would prove an inestimable blessing. We may abhor his conduct, while we can still make generous allowances for the darkness of his mind and of the age in which he lived. It requires infinite wisdom to adjust the balance of human deeds.

Two of the Catholic ecclesiastics, Olmedo and Diaz, were probably unaffected Christians, truly desiring the spiritual renovation of the Indians. They felt deeply the worth of the soul, and did all they could rightly to instruct these unhappy and deeply-wronged natives. They sincerely pitied their sufferings, but deemed it wise that the right eye should be plucked out, and that the right arm should be cut off, rather than that the soul should perish. It is a consoling thought, that "like as a father pitieth his children, so the Lord pitieth them that fear Him; for he knoweth our frame, he remembereth that we are dust." The natives were assembled in their temples; they came together in immense multitudes. The priests, through their interpreter, Aguilar, endeavored to instruct them in the pure doctrines and the sublime mysteries of Christianity. If the natives perceived a marked difference between these precepts and the awful carnage on the field of Ceutla, it was not the first time that principles and practice have been found discordant.

A grand religious ceremony was instituted to commemorate the conversion of the nation. The whole army took a part in the solemnities of the occasion, with all the martial and ecclesiastical pomp which their situation could furnish. The natives in countless multitudes joined the procession, and gazed with astonishment upon the scene. Advancing to the principal pyramidal temple of Tabasco, which was an enormous structure, with a vast area upon its summit, they wound around its sides in the ascent. Upon this lofty platform, beneath the unclouded sun, with thousands of Indians crowding the region around to witness the strange spectacle, a Christian altar was reared, the images of the Savior and of the Virgin were erected, and mass was celebrated. Clouds of incense rose into the still air, and the rich voices of the Spanish soldiers swelled the solemn chant. It must have been an impressive scene. There must have been some there into whose eye the tear of devotion gushed. If there were in that throng—all of whom have long since gone to judgment—one single broken and contrite heart, that was an offering which God could accept. Father Olmedo preached upon the occasion "many good things touching our holy faith." Twenty Indian girls who had been given to the Spanish captains for wives were baptized.

Cortez having thus, in the course of a week, annexed the whole of these new provinces of unknown extent to Spain, and having converted the natives to Christianity, prepared for his departure. The natives, among their propitiatory offerings, had presented to Cortez, as we have mentioned, twenty young and beautiful females whom they had captured from hostile tribes, or who in other ways had become their slaves. Cortez distributed these unenlightened maidens among his captains, having first selected one of the youngest and most beautiful of them, Marina, for his wife. Cortez had a worthy spouse upon his plantation at Cuba. No civil or religious rites sanctioned this unhallowed union; and he was sufficiently instructed to know that he was sinning against the laws of both God and man; but the conscience of this extraordinary adventurer had become involved in labyrinths utterly inexplicable. He seemed to judge that he was doing so much for the cause of Holy Mother Church that his own private sins were of little comparative moment. His many good deeds, he appeared to think, purchased ample indulgence.

But Marina was a noble woman. The relation which she sustained to Cortez did no violence to her instincts or to her conscience. She had never been instructed in the school of Christ. Polygamy was the religion of her land. She deemed herself the honored wife of Cortez, and dreamed not of wrong. Marina was in all respects an extraordinary woman. Nature had done much for her. In person she was exceedingly beautiful. She had winning manners, and a warm and loving heart. Her mind was of a superior order. She very quickly mastered the difficulties of the Castilian tongue, and thus spoke three languages with native fluency—the Mexican, the Yucatanese, and the Spanish. "I am more happy," said she one day, "in being the wife of my lord and master Cortez, and of having a son by him, than if I had been sovereign of all of New Spain."

Her career had been eventful in the extreme. She was the daughter of a rich and powerful cacique, who was tributary to the Emperor of Mexico. Her father died during her infancy, and her mother married again. A son by her new husband gradually estranged the affections of the unnatural mother from her daughter. These feelings increased, till she regarded the child with deep dislike, and secretly gave her away to some slave-drivers, circulating the report that the child was dead. The slave-merchants brought her from her distant home, where the language of Mexico was her native tongue, and sold her to one of the chiefs of Tabasco. Here she acquired the language of Yucatan.

There was much in the energy, magnanimity, fearlessness, and glowing temperament of Cortez to rouse a woman's love. Marina became devotedly attached to him. She watched over his interests with a zeal which never slumbered; and when she became the mother of his son, still more tender ties bound her to the conqueror of her race. In subsequent scenes of difficulty and danger, her acquaintance with the native language, manners, and customs made her an invaluable acquisition to the expedition.

After a few days spent at Tabasco, the hour for departure came.

The boats, decorated with the banner of the cross, and with palm leaves, the symbols of happiness and peace, floated down the beautiful river to the squadron riding at anchor at its mouth. Again spreading the sails, and catching a favorable breeze, the adventurers were wafted rejoicingly on toward the shores of Mexico. The newly-converted natives were left to meditate upon the instructions which they had received—to count the graves of the slain—to heal, as they could, the gory wounds and splintered bones of their friends, still writhing in anguish, and to wail the funeral dirge in the desolate homes of the widow and the orphan. Seldom, in the history of the world, has such a whirlwind of woe so suddenly burst upon any people. How long they continued to cherish a religion introduced by such harbingers we are not informed.

The sun shone brightly on the broad Mexican Gulf, and zephyrs laden with fragrance from the luxuriant shores swelled the flowing sheets.

As the fleet crept along the land, the temples and houses of the natives, and their waving fields of grain, were distinctly visible from the decks. Many a promontory and headland was covered with multitudes of tawny figures, decorated with all the attractions of barbarian splendor, gazing upon the fearful phenomena of the passing ships. Cortez continued his course several hundred miles, sweeping around the shores of this magnificent gulf, until he arrived at the island of San Juan de Ulua. He was seeking this spot, which Grijalva had visited, and here he dropped his anchors in one of the harbors of the empire of Mexico.

CHAPTER IV.

FOUNDING A COLONY.

IT was a beautiful afternoon in April when the fleet sailed majestically into the Mexican bay. Earth, sea, and sky smiled serenely, and all the elements of trouble were lulled into repose. As the ships glided over the smooth waters to their sheltered anchorage, a scene, as of enchantment, opened around the voyagers. In the distance, on grassy slopes, and in the midst of luxuriant groves, the villages and rural dwellings of the natives were thickly scattered. The shores were covered with an eager multitude, contemplating with wonder and awe the sublime spectacle of the fleet.

Hardly were the anchors dropped ere two canoes shot from the shore, filled with natives. The ship in which Cortez sailed was more imposing than the rest, and the banner of Spain floated proudly from its topmast. The Mexicans steered promptly for this vessel, and, with the most confiding frankness, ascended its sides. Two of the persons in these boats were men of high distinction in the Mexican empire. As Marina understood their language perfectly, and the liberated Spanish captive Aguilar was thoroughly acquainted with the language of the Tabascans, there was no difficulty in the interchange of ideas. One of these men was the governor of the province in which Cortez had landed; the other was commander-in-chief of all the military forces in that province. It has been mentioned that Grijalva had previously landed at this spot, and given it the name of San Juan de Ulua. The Mexicans had thus some knowledge of the formidable strangers who were invading the New World, and in various ways tidings, for now the quarter of a century, had been reaching their ears of the appalling power of this new race.

Perhaps to this fact is to be attributed the general and discouraging impression which then prevailed, that a fearful calamity which nothing could avert was impending over the nation; that it was the decree of destiny that a strange race, coming from the rising of the sun, should overwhelm and desolate their country.

The two chiefs brought Cortez a present of bread, fruit, fowls, flowers, and golden ornaments. The interview was conducted by the interchange of the most formal social ceremonies of Mexico and of Spain. Cortez invited his guests to remain and dine. The communication between them was necessarily slow, as Marina interpreted their speech to Aguilar, and Aguilar to Cortez. The Spanish commander, however, thus ascertained the most important facts which he wished to know respecting the great empire of Mexico. He learned that two hundred miles in the interior was situated the capital of the empire, and that a monarch named Montezuma, beloved and revered by his subjects, reigned over the extended realm. The country was divided into provinces, over each of which a governor presided. The province in which Cortez had landed was under the sway of Governor Teutile, who resided about twenty miles in the interior.

Cortez, though uninvited, immediately, with great energy and boldness, landed his whole force upon the beach. He constructed a fortified camp, and planted his heavy artillery upon the surrounding hillocks to sweep all the approaches. Characteristically it is recorded that, having posted their artillery, they *raised an altar*, and not till after that was done did they erect barracks for themselves. The friendly natives aided the Spaniards in building huts, brought them presents of flowers and food, and entered into an active traffic, in which both parties exulted in the great bargains which they made. Thus the Mexicans warmed the vipers who were fatally to sting them.

It was indeed a novel scene, worthy of the pencil of the painter, which that beach presented day after day. Men, women, and children, boys and girls, in all the variety of barbaric costume, thronged the encampment. Mexicans and Spaniards mingled merrily in all the peaceful and joyful confusion of a fair. The rumor of the strange visitors spread far and wide, and each day increasing multitudes were assembled.

The intelligence was speedily communicated to Governor Teutile. With a numerous retinue, he set out from his palace to visit his uninvited guests, and to ascertain their object and purposes. The governor entered the Spanish camp accompanied by the commander-in-chief of all the provincial forces. Each party vied in the external demonstrations of respect and friendship. The eyes of the Spaniards glistened with avarice as Teutile spread before Cortez many valuable ornaments of massive silver and gold, wrought in exquisite workmanship. The sight inflamed them with more intense desires to penetrate a country where such treasures could be obtained. After a splendid repast given by the Spaniards, Cortez said to his visitors,

"I am the subject of Charles V., the most powerful monarch in the world. My sovereign has heard of the greatness and the glory of Montezuma, the Emperor of Mexico. I am sent to his court to convey the respects of my sovereign, to offer suitable presents, and to confer with him upon matters of great moment. It is therefore my desire to proceed immediately to the capital, to accomplish the purposes of my mission."

Teutile could not conceal the uneasiness with which he heard this avowal. He knew that Montezuma and all the most intelligent men of the nation contemplated with dread the power and the encroachments of the Europeans, now so firmly established on the islands of the Caribbean Sea. With embarrassment he replied,

"I hear with pleasure of the magnificence of your sovereign. Our monarch is not less glorious. No earthly king can surpass him in wealth or goodness. You have been but a few days in these realms, and yet you are impatient to be admitted, without delay, into the presence of Montezuma. Our king will doubtless hear with pleasure from your sovereign, and receive his embassador honorably. But it will be first necessary to inform him of your arrival, that he may communicate to you his royal pleasure."

Cortez was exceedingly annoyed by this delay. Deeming it, however, important to secure the friendship of the Mexicans, he consented to wait until the return of the couriers who were immediately to be sent to Montezuma. The natives were not acquainted with the alphabet, but they had in use a sort of *picture writing*, delineating upon fine cotton cloth pictures of scenes which they wished to represent. Teutile requested that his painters might be permitted to take a sketch of the Spaniards and their equipage. Consent being obtained, the painters commenced their work, which they executed with remarkable rapidity and skill. The fleet in the harbor, the encampment upon the shore, the muskets, the artillery, the horses, all were delineated true to life. They were so accurate in the figures and portraits of Cortez and his leading companions that the Spaniards immediately recognized them.

When Cortez observed this remarkable skill, that he might impress Montezuma the more deeply with a sense of his power, he ordered his whole force to be assembled for a military review. The trumpets pealed forth the martial summons which the well-drilled bands so perfectly understood. The troops instantly formed in order of battle. Infantry, artillery, cavalry, all were at their posts. The most intricate and beautiful manœuvres were performed. Martial music contributed its thrilling charms; banners floated in the breeze; helmets, cuirasses, swords, and polished muskets gleamed in the rays of the unclouded sun. Mounted horsemen bounded over the plain in the terrific charge, and the artillerymen, with rapid evolutions, moved to and fro, dragging over the sands their lumbering yet mysterious engines of destruction, whose awful roar and terrific power the Mexicans had not yet witnessed. It was a gorgeous spectacle even to eyes accustomed to such scenes. The Mexicans, in countless thousands, gazed upon it in silent amazement. But when, at the close, Cortez placed his cannon in battery, and ordered a simultaneous discharge, aiming the heavily-shotted guns into the dense forest, the bewilderment of the poor natives passed away into unspeakable terror. They saw the lightning flash, they heard the roar, louder than the heaviest thunders. As the iron storm was shot through the forest, the limbs of the gigantic trees came crashing to the ground. Dense volumes of sulphurous smoke enveloped them. Even the boldest turned pale, and the timid shrieked and fled.

Cortez was much pleased in seeing how deeply he had impressed his visitors with a sense of his power. The painters made a very accurate delineation of the whole scene to be transmitted to Montezuma. They then, with much ceremony, departed.

The police regulations of Mexico were in some respects in advance of that which then prevailed in Europe. For the rapid transmission of intelligence from the remotest bounds of the empire to the capital, well-trained runners were posted, at suitable stations, all along the principal roads. Each man had a short stage, which he passed over with great rapidity, and communicated his message, verbal or written in the picture language, to a fresh runner. Burdens and governmental officers were also rapidly transmitted, in a sort of palanquin, in the same way, from post to post, by relays of men.

A week passed while Cortez remained impatiently in his encampment awaiting an answer to the message sent to Montezuma. The friendly natives, in the mean time, supplied the Spaniards with every thing they could need. By the command of the governor, Teutile, more than a thousand huts of branches of trees and of cotton matting were reared in the vicinity of the encampment for the accommodation of the Mexicans, who, without recompense, were abundantly supplying the table of Cortez and of his troops.

On the eighth day an embassy arrived at the camp from the Mexican capital. Two nobles of the court, accompanied by a retinue of a hundred *men of burden*, laden with magnificent gifts from Montezuma, presented themselves before the pavilion of Cortez. The embassadors saluted the Spanish chieftain with the greatest reverence, bowing before him, and surrounding him with clouds of incense, which arose from waving censers borne by their attendants. The presents which they brought, in silver, in gold, in works of art, utility, and beauty, excited the rapture and the amazement of the Spaniards. There were specimens of workmanship in the precious metals which no

INTERVIEW BETWEEN CORTEZ AND THE EMBASSADORS OF MONTEZUMA.

artists in Europe could rival. A Spanish helmet which had been sent to Montezuma was returned filled with grains of pure gold. These costly gifts were opened before Cortez in lavish abundance, and they gave indications of opulence hitherto undreamed of. After they had been sufficiently examined and admired, one of the embassadors very courteously said,

"Our master is happy to send these tokens of his respect to the King of Spain. He regrets that he can not enjoy an interview with the Spaniards. But the distance of his capital is too great, and the perils of the journey are too imminent to allow of this pleasure. The strangers are therefore requested to return to their own homes with these proofs of the friendly feelings of Montezuma."

Cortez was much chagrined. He earnestly, however, renewed his application for permission to visit the emperor. But the embassadors, as they retired, assured him that another application would be unavailing. They, however, took a few meagre presents of shirts and toys, which alone remained to Cortez, and departed on their journey of two hundred miles, with the reiterated and still more earnest application from Cortez for permission to visit the emperor. It was now evident that the Mexicans had received instructions from the court, and that all were anxious that the Spaniards should leave the country. Though the natives manifested no hostility, they immediately became cold and reserved, and ceased to supply the camp with food. With the Spaniards the charm of novelty was over. Insects annoyed them. They were blistered by the rays of a meridian sun, reflected from the burning sands of the beach. Sickness entered the camp, and thirty died. Disaffection began to manifest itself, and some were anxious to return to Cuba.

But the treasures which had been received from Montezuma, so rich and so abundant, inspired Cortez and his gold-loving companions with the most intense desire to penetrate an empire of so much opulence. They, however, waited patiently ten days, when the embassadors again returned. As before, they came laden with truly imperial gifts. The gold alone of the ornaments which they brought was valued by the Spaniards at more than fifty thousand dollars. The message from Montezuma was, however, still more peremptory than the first. He declared that he could not permit the Spaniards to approach his capital. Cortez, though excessively vexed, endeavored to smother the outward expression of his irritation. He gave the embassadors a courteous response, but, turning to his officers, he said,

"This is truly a rich and a powerful prince. Yet it shall go hard but we will one day pay him a visit in his capital."

"At this moment," says Diaz, "the bell tolled for the Ave Maria, and all of us fell upon our knees before the holy cross. The Mexican noblemen being very inquisitive to know the meaning of this, Cortez hinted to the reverend father Olmedo the propriety of a sermon, such as should convey to them the truths of our holy faith. Father Olmedo accordingly preached, like an excellent theologian which he was, explaining the mysteries of the cross, at the sight of which the evil beings they worshiped as gods fled away. These subjects, and much more, he dilated upon. It was perfectly explained to the Mexicans and understood by them, and they promised to relate all they had seen and heard to their sovereign. He also declared to them that among the principal objects of our mission thither were those of putting a stop to human sacrifices, injustices, and idolatrous worship; and then, presenting them with an image of our Holy Virgin, with her son in her arms, he desired them to take it with them, to venerate it, and to plant crosses similar to that before them in their temples."

The embassadors again retired with dignity and with courtesy, yet with reserve indicative of deep displeasure at the pertinacity of the Spaniards. That night every hut of the natives was abandoned. When the morning sun arose, silence and solitude reigned upon the spot which had so recently witnessed the life and the clamor of an innumerable multitude. Cortez and his companions were left alone. The long hours of the tropical day passed slowly, and no native approached the encampment. No food was to be obtained. Not only was all friendly intercourse thus suspended, but the Spaniards had much reason to fear that preparations were making for an assault. The murmuring in the camp increased. Two parties were formed: one party were in favor of returning to Cuba, affirming that it was madness to think of the subjugation by force of arms of so mighty an empire with so feeble an armament. One of the generals, Diego de Ordaz, was deputed by the disaffected to communicate these sentiments to Cortez, and to assure him that it was the general voice of the army.

The shrewdness of this extraordinary man was peculiarly conspicuous in this crisis. He promptly, and apparently with cordiality, assented to their views, and began to make arrangements to relinquish the enterprise. Orders were issued to commence the re-embarkation.

While thus dissimulating, he roused his friends to effort, and secretly employed all his powers to excite a mutiny in the camp against a return. Every motive was plied to stimulate the bold and the avaricious to persevere in an undertaking where glory and wealth held out such attractions. His emissaries were completely successful. The whole camp was in a ferment. Before the sun went down, a large party of the soldiers surrounded his tent, as in open mutiny. They declared that, having entered upon a majestic enterprise, it was poltroonery to abandon it upon the first aspect of danger; that they were determined to persevere, and that, if Cortez wished to return with the cowards to Cuba, they would instantly choose another general to guide them in the career of glory upon which they had entered.

Cortez was delighted with the success of his stratagem. He, however, affected surprise, and declared that his orders for re-embarking were issued from the persuasion that the troops wished to return; that, to gratify them, he had been willing to sacrifice his own private judgment. He assured the mutineers that it afforded him the highest gratification to find that they were true Castilians, with minds elevated to the accomplishment of heroic deeds. He affirmed that before such strong arms and bold hearts all peril would vanish. The applause with which this speech was greeted was so long and enthusiastic that even the murmurers were soon induced to join the acclamations. Thus adroitly Cortez again enthroned himself as the undisputed chieftain of an enthusiastic band.

He decided immediately to establish a settlement on the sea-coast as the nucleus of a colony. From that point as the basis of operations, he would, with the terrors of artillery and cavalry, boldly penetrate the interior. He assembled the principal officers of the army, and by their suffrages elected the magistrates and a council for the new colony. He skillfully so arranged it that all the magistrates chosen were his warm partisans.

The council assembled for the organization of the government. As soon as the assembly was convened, Cortez asked permission to enter it. Bowing with the most profound respect before the new government thus organized, that he might set an example of the most humble and submissive obedience, he addressed them in the following terms:

"By the establishment of the colony and the organization of the colonial government, this august tribunal is henceforth invested with supreme jurisdiction, and is clothed with the authority, and represents the person of the sovereign. I accordingly present myself before you with the same dutiful fidelity as if I were addressing my royal master. The safety of this colony, threatened by the hostility of a mighty empire, depends upon the subordination and discipline preserved among the troops. But my right to command is derived from a commission granted by the Governor of Cuba. As that commission has been long since revoked, my right to command may well be questioned. It is of the utmost importance, in the present condition of affairs, that the commander-in-chief should not act upon a dubious title. There is now required the most implicit obedience to orders, and the army can not act with efficiency if it has any occasion to dispute the powers of its general.

"Moved by these considerations, I now resign into your hands, as the representatives of the sovereign, all my authority. As you alone have the right to choose, and the power to confer full jurisdiction, upon you it devolves to choose some one, in the king's name, to guide the army in its future operations. For my own part, such is my zeal in the service in which we are engaged, that I would most cheerfully take up a pike with the same hand which lays down the general's truncheon, and convince my fellow-soldiers that, though accustomed to command, I have not forgotten how to obey."

Thus saying, he laid his commission from Velasquez upon the table, and after kissing his truncheon, delivered it to the chief magistrate and withdrew. This was consummate acting. The succeeding steps were all previously arranged. He was immediately elected, by unanimous suffrage, chief justice of the colony, and captain general of the army. His commission was ordered to be made out in the name of Charles V. of Spain, and was to continue in force until the royal pleasure should be farther known. The troops were immediately assembled and informed of the resolve. They ratified it with unbounded applause. The air resounded with acclamations, and all vowed obedience, even to death, to the authority of Cortez. Thus adroitly this bold adventurer shook off his dependence upon Velasquez, and assumed the dignity of an independent governor, responsible only to his sovereign.

There were a few adherents of Velasquez who remonstrated against these unprecedented measures. Cortez, with characteristic energy, seized them and placed them in imprisonment, loaded with chains, on board one of the ships. This rigor overawed and silenced the rest. Cortez, however, soon succeeded, by flattering attentions and by gifts, in securing a cordial reconciliation with his opponents. He was now strong in undisputed authority.

In the midst of these events, one day five Indians of rank came, in rather a mysterious manner, to the camp, and solicited an interview with Cortez. They represented themselves as envoys from the chief of Zempoalla, a large town at no great distance. This chief reigned over the powerful nation of Totonacs. His people had been conquered by Montezuma, and annexed to the Mexican empire. They were restive under the yoke, and would gladly avail themselves of an alliance with the Spaniards to regain their independence.

Cortez listened eagerly to this statement. It presented just the opportunity which he desired. He saw at once that by exciting civil war, and arraying one portion of the empire against another, he might accomplish his ends. He also judged that, in an empire so vast, there must be other provinces where disaffection could be excited. He therefore received these envoys most graciously, and promised very soon to visit their metropolis.

The spot where Cortez had landed was not a good location for the establishment of a city. A party was sent along the coast to seek a better harbor for the ships and a more eligible site for the city. At the expiration of twelve days the party returned, having discovered a fine harbor and fertile soil at a little village called Quiabislan, about forty miles to the northward. This village was fortunately but a few miles distant from Zempoalla. Most of the heavy guns were re-embarked, and the fleet was ordered to coast along the shore to the appointed rendezvous at Quiabislan. Then, heading his troops, he set out on a bold march across the country to meet his fleet, arranging to pass through Zempoalla by the way.

The beauty of the country through which

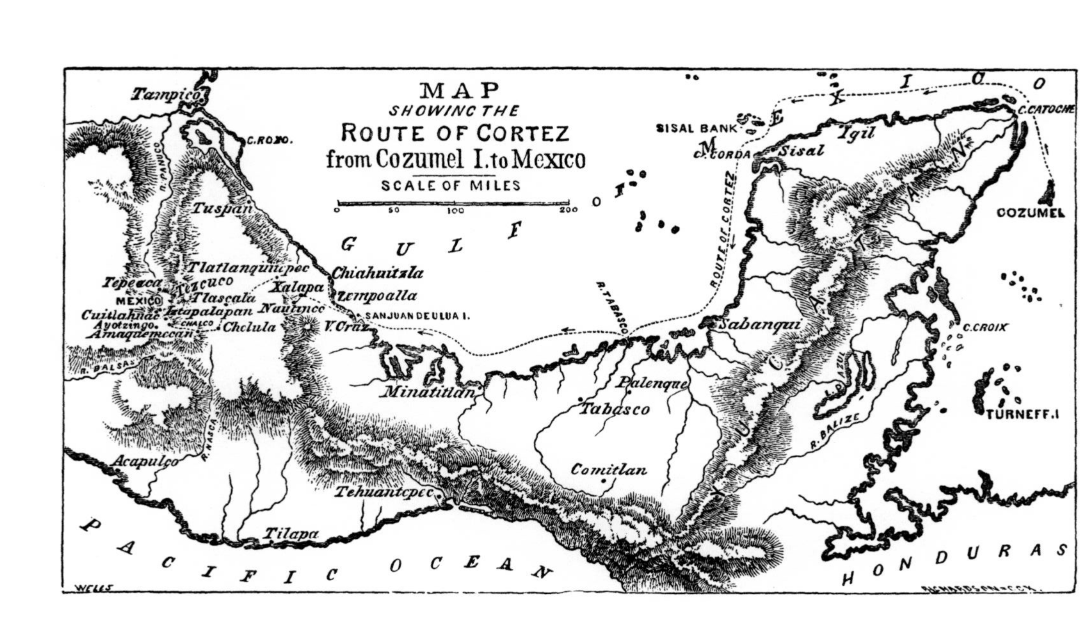
MAP
SHOWING THE
ROUTE OF CORTEZ
from Cozumel I. to Mexico
SCALE OF MILES
0
50
100
200
Tampico
C. ROXO.
R. PANUCO
Tuspan
Tlatlanquitepec
Tepeaca
Tezcuco
MEXICO
Tlascala
Xalapa
Chiahuitzla
Zempoalla
Cuitlahnac
Iztapalapan
Nautinco
Ayotzingo.
CHALCO
Amaquemecan
Cholula
V. Cruz
SANJUAN DE ULUA I.
R. BALSAS
R. NASCA
Acapulco
Minatitlan
Tehuantepec
Tilapa
PACIFIC OCEAN
GULF OF MEXICO
R. TABASCO
ROUTE OF CORTEZ
SISAL BANK
C. CORDA
Sisal
Igil
C. CATOCHE
COZUMEL
Sabanqui
Palenque
Tabasco
Comitlan
YUCATAN
L. AZUL
R. BALIZE
C. CROIX
TURNEFF. I
HONDURAS
WELLS

they marched entranced the hearts even of these stern warriors. They were never weary of expressing their delight in view of the terrestrial paradise which they had discovered. When the Spaniards had arrived within three miles of Zempoalla, a delegation met them from the city, accompanied by a vast concourse of men and women. The adventurers were greeted with courteous words, and gifts of gold, and fruits, and flowers. The natives possessed many attractions of person, and their frank and friendly manners were peculiarly winning. A singular degree of mental refinement was to be seen in their passionate love of flowers, with which they adorned their persons, and which bloomed, in the utmost profusion, around their dwellings. Cortez and his steed were almost covered with wreaths and garlands of roses, woven by the fair hands of his newly-found friends.

The Spaniards were quite amazed in entering the city of Zempoalla. They found a beautiful town, with streets perfectly clean—for they had no beasts of burden—lined with spacious stone houses, and shaded with ornamental trees. These paved streets were kept almost as free from litter as a parlor floor, and they were thronged with, apparently, a refined and happy people. A tropical sun, whose rays were tempered by the ocean breeze, fell warmly upon them during all the months of the year. Soil of astonishing fertility supplied them abundantly with food, while a genial climate invited them to indulgence and repose. At first glance it would seem that the doom of Adam's fall had not yet reached the dwellings of Zempoalla. A few hours' residence in the city, however, conclusively proved that here, as elsewhere, man is born to mourn.

As Cortez entered the gates of the city, he was met and welcomed with great pomp by the cacique of Zempoalla. He was excessively corpulent, but very polite and highly polished in his manners. Marina and Aguilar acted as interpreters.

"I am come," said Cortez, "from the ends of the earth. I serve a monarch who is powerful, and whose goodness equals his power. He has sent me hither, that I may give some account of the inhabitants of this part of the world. He has commanded me to do good to all men, and particularly to aid the oppressed and to punish their oppressors. To you, Lord of Zempoalla, I offer my services. Whatever you may command, I and my troops will cheerfully perform."

The cacique of Zempoalla replied,

"Gracious stranger, I can not sufficiently commend your benevolence, and none can stand more in need of it. You see before you a man wearied out with unmerited wrongs. I and my people are crushed and trodden under foot by the most tyrannical power upon earth. We were once an independent and a happy people, but the prosperity of the Totonacs is now destroyed. The power of our nobles is gone. We are robbed of the produce of our fields. Our sons are torn from us for sacrifices, and our daughters for slaves.

"The Mexicans are our conquerors and oppressors. They heap these calamities upon us, robbing us of our substance, and despoiling us of our children. In the pride of aggression, they have marched from conquest to conquest, till they gather tribute from every land. And now, mighty warrior, we implore of thy strength and kindness that thou wouldst enable us to resist these tyrants, and deliver us from their exactions."

Cortez warily replied: "I will gladly aid you, but let us not be rash. I will dwell with you a while, and whenever I shall see a suitable occasion to punish your enemies and to relieve you from their impositions, you may rely upon my aid to humble their pride and power."

The rugged army of Cortez then advanced through the streets of Zempoalla to the spacious court-yard of the temple assigned for their accommodation. As in solid column, with floating banners and bugle notes, they paraded the streets, headed by the cavalry of sixteen horses, animals the Totonacs had never seen before, and followed by the lumbering artillery—instruments, in the eyes of the Totonacs, of supernatural power—which, with thunder roar, sped lightning bolts, the natives gazed with admiration upon the imposing spectacle, and the air resounded with their applause.

The next morning Cortez, with most of his army, continued his march some twelve miles farther to meet his fleet at Quiabislan. The cacique hospitably sent with him four hundred *men of burden* to convey his baggage. The spot which had been selected as the site of the new town, which was to be the capital of the Spanish colony, met the approbation of Cortez. He immediately commenced erecting huts and surrounding the town with fortifications of sufficient strength to resist any assault from the natives. Every man in the army, the officers as well as the soldiers, engaged laboriously in this work. No one toiled in this enterprise with more patient endurance than the extraordinary commander of this extraordinary band. The Totonacs from Zempoalla and Quiabislan, encouraged by their caciques, also lent their aid to the enterprise with hearty good will. Thousands of hands were thus employed; provisions flowed into the camp in all abundance, and the works proceeded with great rapidity. The vicinity was densely populated, and large numbers of the listless natives, women and children, were attracted to the spot to witness the busy scene, so novel and so exciting.

But such proceedings could not escape the vigilance of the officers of Montezuma. In the midst of this state of things, suddenly one day a strange commotion was witnessed in the crowd, and the natives, both people and chiefs, gave indications of great terror. Five strangers appeared—tall, imposing men, with bouquets of flowers in their hands, and followed by obsequious attendants. Haughtily these strangers passed through the place, looking sternly upon the Spaniards, without deigning to address them either by a word or a gesture. They were lords from the court of Montezuma. Their power was invincible and terrible. They had witnessed with their own eyes these rebellious indications of the subjects of Mexico. The chiefs of the Totonacs turned pale with consternation. All this was explained to Cortez by Marina.

The Totonac chiefs were imperiously summoned to appear immediately before the lords of Montezuma. Like terrified children they obeyed. Soon they returned, trembling, to Cortez, and informed him that the Mexican lords were indignant at the support which they had afforded the Spaniards, contrary to the express will of their emperor, and that they demanded as the penalty twenty young men and twenty young women of the Totonacs, to be offered in sacrifice to their gods.

Cortez assumed an air of indignation and of authority as he eagerly availed himself of this opportunity of promoting an open rupture between the Totonacs and the Mexicans. He declared that he would never consent to any such abominable practices of heathenism. He haughtily commanded the Totonac chiefs immediately to arrest the lords of Montezuma, and throw them into prison. The poor chiefs were appalled beyond measure at the very idea of an act so irrevocable and so unpardonable.

They had long been accustomed to consider Montezuma as possessing power which nothing on earth could resist. Montezuma swayed the sceptre of a Cæsar, and bold indeed must he be who would venture to brave his wrath.

But, on the other hand, they had already offended beyond hope of pardon by entertaining the intruders contrary to the positive command of their sovereign. Twenty of their sons and daughters were to bleed upon the altars of sacrifice. Their only hope was now in Cortez. Should he abandon them, they were ruined hopelessly. They deemed it possible that, with the thunder and the lightning at his command, he might be able to set at defiance that mighty Mexican power which had hitherto been found invincible.

In this dreadful dilemma, they yielded to the inexorable demand of Cortez, and tremblingly arrested the Mexican lords. The Rubicon was now passed. The Totonacs were from that moment the abject slaves of Cortez. Their only protection from the most awful doom was in his strong arm, and their persons, their property, their all, were entirely at his disposal.

Cortez then condescended to perform a deed of cunning and of perfidy which has left a stain upon his character which never can be washed away. In the night he ordered one of his people secretly to assist two of the Mexican lords in their escape. They were privately brought into his presence. With guileful words, which ought to have blistered his tongue, he declared that they, by their arrest, had received insult and outrage from the Totonacs, which he sincerely regretted, and would gladly have prevented. He assured them of the great pleasure which it afforded him to aid them in their escape. He promised to do every thing in his power to secure the release of the others, and wished them to return to the court of their monarch, and assure him of the friendly spirit of the Spaniards, of which this act was to be a conspicuous proof. He then sent six strong rowers to convey them secretly in a boat beyond the reach of pursuit. The next morning, in the same guileful way, all the rest were liberated, and sent with a similar message to the court of Montezuma.

Such was the treachery with which Cortez rewarded his faithful allies. With perfidy so detestable, he endeavored to foment civil discord in the empire of Montezuma, pretending to be himself the friend of each of the parties whose hostility he had excited, and ready to espouse either side which might appear most available for the promotion of his ambitious plans. History has no language too severe to condemn an action so utterly abominable. It is treason to virtue to speak mildly of atrocious crime.

Cortez named the infant city he was erecting The Rich City of the True Cross, *Villa Rica de la Vera Cruz.* "The two principles of avarice and enthusiasm," says Robertson, "which prompted the Spaniards in all their enterprises in the New World, seem to have concurred in suggesting the name which Cortez bestowed on his infant settlement." This city was a few miles north of the present city of Vera Cruz.

While Cortez was busily employed in laying the foundations of his colony, and gathering around him native aid in preparation for a march into the interior, another embassy from the court of Montezuma appeared in the busy streets of Vera Cruz. The Mexican emperor, alarmed by the tidings he received of the persistent boldness of the Spaniards, and of their appalling and supernatural power, deemed it wise to accept the courtesy which had been offered him in the liberation of his imprisoned lords, and to adopt a conciliatory policy. The Totonacs were amazed by this evidence that even the mighty Montezuma was overawed by the power of the Spaniards. This greatly increased their veneration for their European allies.

CHAPTER V.

THE TLASCALANS SUBJUGATED.

THE Totonacs were now exceedingly exultant. They were unwearied in extolling their allies, and in proclaiming their future independence of their Mexican conquerors. They urged other neighboring provinces to join them, and become the vassals of the omnipotent Spaniards. They raised a strong army, which they placed under the command of Cortez to obey his bidding. To strengthen the bonds of alliance, the cacique of Zempoalla selected eight of the most beautiful maidens of his country, all of the first families, to be united in marriage to the Spanish generals. Cortez courteously but decisively informed the chief that, before such union could be consummated, these maidens must all renounce idolatry and be baptized. The Totonacs, without much apparent reluctance, yielded. Emboldened by this success, Cortez now made very strenuous efforts to induce the chief and all the tribe to abandon their idols and the cruel rites of heathenism, and to accept in their stead the symbols of Christianity.

But upon this point the cacique was inflexible. "We honor your friendship, noble Cortez," he firmly replied, "and we are grateful to you for the generous interest you take in our welfare; but the gods are greater than man. Earthly benefactors are but the ministers of their favor. Gratitude to the gods is our first duty. Health, plenty, all blessings are from their bounty. We dread their anger more than the displeasure of the mightiest of men. Should we offend them, inevitable destruction will overwhelm me and my people."

Cortez was provoked by such obstinacy. He was incapable of appreciating the nobility of these sentiments, and of perceiving that such minds needed but instruction to lead them to reverence the true God. The sincere idolater, who worships according to the little knowledge he has, is immeasurably elevated, in dignity of character, above the mere nominal Christian, who knows the true God, and yet disregards him. But Cortez, inspired by fanatic zeal, treated these men, who deserved tender consideration, with insult and contempt. He resolved

DESTROYING THE IDOLS AT ZEMPOALLA

recklessly to demolish their idols, and to compel the Totonacs to receive in exchange the images of Rome.

He immediately assembled his soldiers, and thus addressed them: "Soldiers! We are Spaniards. We inherit from our ancestors the love of our holy faith. Let us prostrate these vile images. Let us plant the cross, and call the heathen to the feet of that holy symbol. Heaven will never smile upon our enterprise if we countenance the atrocities of heathenism. For my part, I am resolved that these pagan idols shall be destroyed this very hour, even if it cost me my life."

The fanaticism of the Spaniards was now effectually roused. In solid column, a strong division marched toward one of the most imposing of the Totonac temples. The alarm spread wildly through the thronged streets of Zempoalla. The whole population seized their arms to defend their gods. A scene of fearful confusion ensued. Firmly the inflexible Spaniards strode on. Fifty men ascended the winding stairs to the summit of the pyramidal temple, tore down the massive wooden idols, and tumbled them into the streets. They then collected the mutilated fragments, and burned them to ashes. The Indians looked on in dismay, with tears and groans.

The heathen temple was then emptied, swept, and garnished. The Totonac chiefs, and the priests clotted with the blood of their brutal sacrifices, now docile as children, obeyed obsequiously the demands of the haughty reformer. He ordered these unenlightened pagan priests to have their heads shorn, to be dressed in the white robes of the Catholic priesthood, and, with lighted candles in their hands, they were constrained to assist in performing the rites of the papal Church. An image of the Virgin was installed in the shrine which had been polluted by all the horrid orgies of pagan abominations. Mass was celebrated upon the altar where human hearts, gory and quivering, had for ages been offered in awful sacrifice. The prayers and the chants of Christianity ascended from the spot where idolaters had slain their victims and implored vengeance upon their foes.

Cortez then himself earnestly and eloquently harangued the people, assuring them that henceforth the Spaniards and the Totonacs were Christian brothers, and that under the protection of the Holy Virgin, the mother of Christ, they would both certainly be blessed.

Violent as were these deeds, it is undeniable that they ushered in a blessed change. The very lowest and most corrupt form of Christianity is infinitely superior to the most refined creations of paganism. The natives gradually recovered from their terror. They gazed with admiration upon the pageant of the mass, with its gorgeous accompaniments of incense, music, embroidered robes, and solemn processions. The Spanish historians who witnessed the scene record that many of the Indians were so overcome with pious emotion, in thus beholding, for the first time, the mysteries of Christianity, that they freely wept. No more resistance was made. The Totonacs, thus easily converted, apparently with cheerfulness exchanged the bloody and hideous idols of Mexico for the more attractive and more merciful idols of Rome. Let not this remark be attributed to want of candor; for no one can deny that, to these uninstructed natives, it was merely an exchange of idols.

Cortez had now been in Mexico nearly three months. Every moment had been occupied in the accomplishment of objects which he deemed of fundamental importance. He was, however, evidently somewhat embarrassed respecting the validity of his title to command. It was at least doubtful whether the king would recognize the authority of a colony established in so novel a manner. Cortez also well knew that Velasquez would apply to his sovereign for redress for the injuries which he had received. The danger was by no means small that, by the command of the king, Cortez would be degraded and punished as a usurper of power.

Before commencing his march into the interior, he deemed it of the utmost importance to take every possible precaution against this danger. He influenced the magistrates of Vera Cruz to address a letter to the Spanish sovereign in justification of the course which had been pursued, and to implore the king to ratify what had been done in his name, and to confirm Cortez in the supreme command. Cortez also wrote himself a long and labored letter to the Emperor Charles V., full of protestations of loyalty and of zeal for the wealth and the renown of the Spanish court. To add weight to his letter, it was accompanied by as rich treasures from the New World as he had thus far been able to accumulate. Such was the ascendency which this extraordinary man had attained over the minds of his associates, and so confident were they in their anticipations of boundless wealth, that all the soldiers, without a murmur, at the suggestion of Cortez, relinquished their part of the public treasure, that the whole might be sent to the king. Two of the chief magistrates of the colony, Portocarrero and Montejo, were sent in one of the two vessels which were fitted out to Spain to convey these letters and presents. They were directed not to stop at the island of Cuba, lest they should be detained by Velasquez. Ere they embarked, mass was celebrated and prayers were offered for a prosperous voyage. It was now the month of July, 1519.

Just after the vessels had sailed, Cortez was much disturbed by a dangerous conspiracy which broke out in the camp. Some of the disaffected, who had been silenced, but not reconciled, with great secresy matured a plan for seizing one of the brigantines and making their escape to Cuba. The conspirators had actually gone on board the vessel, and were ready to weigh the anchor and spread the sails, when one of the number repented of his treachery, and disclosed the plot to Cortez.

The stern chieftain immediately went himself on board the vessel. The crime was too palpable to be denied. He ordered all to be seized and brought on shore. Cortez resolved to punish with a severity which should intimidate against any renewal of a similar attempt. The two ringleaders were immediately put to death. The pilot had one of his feet cut off. Two of the sailors received two hundred lashes. The rest were spared.

It is recorded that Cortez, as he was ratifying this sentence, gave a deep sigh, and exclaimed,

"How happy is he who is not able to write, and is thereby prevented from signing the death-warrants of men!"

But this development of disaffection disturbed Cortez exceedingly. He was about to march two hundred miles into the interior. It would be necessary to leave a garrison at Vera Cruz. The fleet would be lying idly at anchor in the harbor. A more successful attempt might be made during his absence; and Velasquez, informed thus of his position, might easily send, from the powerful colony of Cuba, a force sufficient to take possession of Vera Cruz, and thus leave Cortez in the interior but a desperate adventurer, wandering in the midst of hostile nations. In this emergence, he came to the decision, of almost unparalleled boldness, to *destroy the fleet!* He would thus place himself in a distant land, with but five hundred men, hopelessly cut off from all retreat, and exposed to assault from exasperated nations numbering many millions.

This plan was no sooner conceived than executed. He assembled his principal friends privately, and informed them of his determination.

"We shall thus," said he, "gain all the sailors for soldiers, and the men, having no possibility of escape, must either conquer or die."

While most of the soldiers were employed at Zempoalla, the ships were dismantled of every movable article, and they were then scuttled and sunk. In a few hours the majestic ocean rose and fell in silent solitude where the fleet had so proudly floated. One small vessel only was left.

When the soldiers heard of this desperate deed, they were struck with consternation. They were apparently now forever separated from friends and home. In case of disaster, escape was impossible and destruction sure. Murmurs of indignation, loud and deep, began to rise against Cortez. He immediately gathered his troops around him, and, by his peculiar tact, soothed their anger, and won them to approval of his course. They at once saw that murmurs would now be of no avail; that their destiny was henceforth entirely dependent upon their obedience to their leader. It was evident to all that the least insubordination, in the position of peril in which they were placed, would lead to inevitable ruin. Cortez closed his speech with the following forcible words:

"As for me, I have chosen my part. I will remain here while there is one to bear me company. If there be any so craven as to shrink from sharing the danger of our glorious enterprise, let them go home. There is still one vessel left. Let them take that and return to Cuba. They can tell there how they have deserted their commander and their comrades, and can wait patiently till we return, loaded with the treasures of the Mexicans."

These excitable men were roused to enthusiasm by this speech. One general shout arose, "To Mexico! to Mexico!" Cortez now made vigorous preparations for his march, uninvited and even forbidden, to the capital of Montezuma. All was alacrity in the camp, and the Totonac allies were as zealous in their preparations as were the Spaniards.

On the 15th of August, 1519, commenced this ever-memorable march. The force of Cortez consisted of four hundred Spaniards, fifteen horses, and seven pieces of artillery. The small remainder of his troops, some being sick or otherwise disabled, were left in garrison at Vera Cruz. The cacique of the Totonacs also furnished him with an army of two thousand three hundred men. Of these, two hundred were what were called *men of burden*, trained to carry heavy loads and to perform all arduous labor. These men were invaluable in carrying the luggage and in dragging the heavy artillery. Cortez assembled his forces at Zempoalla. At the moment of their departure, he called all the Spaniards around him, and addressed them in a devout speech.

"The blessed Savior," said he, "will give us victory. We have now no other security than the favor of God and our own stout hearts."

The morning was serene and cloudless when the army commenced its march, which led to scenes of unparalleled cruelty and of blood. Just as the advance guard was leaving, a messenger brought the intelligence that a strange vessel was seen cruising off the coast near Vera Cruz. Cortez was alarmed, being apprehensive that it was some ship belonging to a fleet sent against him by Velasquez. He immediately set off with a small party of horse toward the shore. A boat left the vessel and landed four men. Cortez seized them, and learned that this ship was sent with two others, conveying two hundred and seventy soldiers. The Governor of Jamaica having learned of the expedition of Cortez, had sent this embassy to take possession of the country, and to inform Cortez that, by a royal commission from the sovereign, the Governor of Jamaica was entitled to have authority over the whole coast. Cortez impressed the men as soldiers, and sent them to be added to his army. Hoping to get a few more, he hid, with his guard, for a whole night behind some sand-hills, expecting that others might land to look for their lost comrades. Being disappointed in this expectation, he resorted to a stratagem to lure others on shore. Four of his men were dressed in the clothes of the prisoners, and sent to the coast to make signals. A boat was soon seen making for the shore; but, as soon as three had landed, some suspicion excited the fears of the rest, and they pushed off from the beach. The three were, however, instantly secured, and were immediately sent to join their companions in the ranks. Cortez thus obtained an important re-enforcement of seven Spaniards.

Delaying no longer, the whole army was speedily on the march. For two days they moved gayly along through an enchanting country of luxuriant foliage, waving grain, flowers, and perfume. They encountered no opposition. Indian villages were thickly scattered around, and scenery of surpassing magnificence and loveliness was continually opening before their eyes. On the evening of the second day they arrived at the beautiful town of Jalapa, which was filled with the rural residences of the wealthy natives, and whose elevated site commanded a prospect in which the beautiful and the sublime were most lavishly blended.

Still continuing their march through a well-settled country, as they ascended the gradual slope of the Cordilleras, on the fourth day they arrived at Naulinco. This was a large and populous town, containing many massive temples, whose altars were ever crimsoned with human gore. The adventurers were received here, however, with great kindness. The sight of these heathen temples inspired Cortez, as usual, with intense zeal to convert the natives to Christianity. Time pressed, and it was not safe to indulge in delay. The Indians were bewildered rather than instructed by the exhortations of the Spanish priests. They, however, consented that Cortez should rear a large cross in the centre of their market-place as a memorial of his visit. The enthusiastic Spaniard devoutly hoped that the sight of the cross alone would excite the devotion of the natives.

They had now ascended far up the gentle ascent of the Cordilleras, and were entering the defiles of the mountains. Here they encountered rugged paths, and fierce storms of wind and sleet. A weary march of three days brought them to the high and extended table-land so characteristic of this country, seven thousand feet above the level of the sea. Here they found a fertile and flowery savanna extending before them for many leagues. The country was highly cultivated, and luxuriantly adorned with hedges, with groves, with waving fields of maize, and with picturesque towns and villages. God did indeed seem to smile upon these reckless adventurers. Thus far their march had been as a delightful holiday excursion.

They soon arrived at Tlatlanquitepec. It was even more populous and improving in its architecture than Zempoalla. The stone houses were spacious and comfortable. Thirteen massive temples testified to the religious fervor of the people. But here they witnessed the most appalling indications of the horrid atrocities of pagan idolatry. They found, piled in order, as they judged, one hundred thousand skulls of human victims who had been offered in sacrifice to their gods.* There was a Mexican garrison stationed in this place, but not sufficiently strong to resist the invaders. They, however, gave Cortez a very cold reception, and endeavored to discourage him from advancing by glowing descriptions of the wealth and power of the monarch whose displeasure he was incurring. These developments, however, rather incited anew the zeal of the Spaniards. Cortez, with commendable zeal, again made vigorous but unavailing efforts to induce these benighted pagans to renounce their cruel and bloodstained idols, and accept the religion of Jesus. Poorly as Cortez was instructed in the doctrines and

* "Near some temples were laid numbers of human skeletons, so arranged that they could be counted with ease and certainty. I am convinced, from my own observation, that there were above a hundred thousand. I repeat it, I am sure that there were more than a hundred thousand."—*Bernal Diaz*, p. 91.

the precepts of the Gospel, Christianity, even as darkly discerned by his mind, was infinitely superior to the sanguinary religious rites of these idolaters.

"We come," said he, firmly, to the chiefs and the principal personages of the town, "from a distant country, to warn the great Montezuma to desist from human sacrifices, and all outrages upon his own vassals or his neighbors, and to require from him submission to our monarch; and I now require you, all who hear me, to renounce your human sacrifices, cannibal feasts, and other abominable practices, for such is the command of our Lord God, whom we adore, who gives us life and death, and who is to raise us up to heaven."

The natives, however, clung to the debasing faith of their fathers. The zeal of Cortez was roused. He regarded the hideous idols as representatives of devils, whom it was right, with any violence, to overthrow. He was just about ordering an onslaught upon the temples with sword and hatchet, when the prudent Father Olmedo dissuaded him.

"By introducing our religion thus violently," said this truly good man, "we shall but expose the sacred symbol of the cross and the image of the Blessed Virgin to insult as soon as we shall have departed. We must wait till we can instruct their dark minds, so that from the heart they may embrace our faith."

And here let us record the full and the cordial admission, that the Roman Catholic Church, notwithstanding its corruptions, has sent out into the wilds of heathenism as devoted Christians as the world has ever seen.

After a rest in this city of five days, the route was again commenced. The road wound picturesquely along the banks of a broad and tranquil stream, fringed with an unbroken line of Indian villages. Some twenty leagues of travel brought them to the large town of Xalacingo. Here they met with friendly treatment. They were now on the frontiers of a very powerful nation, called the Tlascalans, who, by their fierce and warlike habits, had thus far succeeded in resisting the aggressions of the Mexicans. The whole nation was organized into a camp, and thus, though many bloody battles had been fought, the Tlascalans maintained their independence.

Cortez was quite sanguine that he should be able to form an alliance with this people. He therefore decided to rest his army for a few days, while an embassy should be sent to the Tlascalan capital to solicit permission to pass through their country, and gently to intimate an alliance. Four Zempoallans of lofty rank were selected as embassadors. In accordance with the custom of the country, they were dressed in official costume, with flowing mantles, and each bearing arrows tipped with *white* feathers, the symbol of peace.

But the Tlascalans had heard of the arrival of the Spaniards upon the coast, of their ships, "armed with thunder and clad with wings," of their fearful war-horses, and of their weapons of destruction of almost supernatural power. They had also heard of the violence with which they had assailed the gods of the country. The principal lords had already assembled in debate to decide upon the course to be pursued should these formidable strangers approach their territory. It was determined to oppose them with all the energies of artifice and of force. The embassadors were accordingly seized and imprisoned, and preparations were made to sacrifice them to their gods. They, however, fortunately made their escape and returned to Cortez.

The Spanish chieftain, disappointed but not

intimidated by this result, made prompt arrangements to force his way through the Tlascalan territory. Waving the sacred banner of the Church before his troops, he exclaimed,

"Spaniards! follow boldly the standard of the Holy Cross. Through this we shall conquer."

"On! on!" was the enthusiastic response of the soldiers. "In God alone we place our trust."

The march of a few miles brought them to an extended wall of solid masonry, built, like the great wall of China, to protect the territory of the Tlascalans from invasion. Though the entrance gate was so constructed that a small army stationed there might have made very powerful resistance, for some reason the Tlascalan force had been withdrawn. The army boldly pressed in, and advanced rapidly, yet using all caution to guard against an ambuscade. They had not proceeded far, however, before they met a large force of the Indians, who attacked them with the utmost fury, and with a degree of military skill and discipline which greatly surprised the Spaniards. Two of the horses were killed, and several of the Spaniards wounded. For a time the situation of the invaders was very precarious; but Cortez soon brought up the artillery, and opened a destructive fire upon the unprotected foe. The thunder of the guns, which the Tlascalans had never heard before, and the horrid carnage of the grape-shot sweeping through their ranks, compelled the warlike natives at last, though slowly and sullenly, to retire. There was, however, no confusion in their retreat. They retired in good order, ever presenting a bold front to their pursuers. Cortez estimated the number of the enemy engaged in this battle at six thousand.

The retiring Tlascalans took with them or destroyed all the provisions which the country afforded; but, notwithstanding this, "their dogs," one of the historians of the expedition records, "which we caught when they returned to their habitations at night, afforded us a very good supper."

It was now the end of September. The army of Cortez had been gradually increased by recruits from among the natives to three thousand. Immediately after this first battle with the Tlascalans, the whole army was assembled to offer thanks to God for the victory, and to implore his continued protection. The soldiers, with the fresh blood of the Tlascalans hardly washed from their hands, partook of the sacrament of the Lord's Supper according to the rites of the Roman Catholic Church.

The army now marched in close order. The Totonac allies, as well as the Spaniards, were drilled to perfect discipline, and all were inspired with intense zeal. With characteristic caution Cortez chose every night his place of halting, and with great vigilance fortified his encampment. There was something truly chivalrous in the magnanimity displayed by these barbarians. They seemed to scorn the idea of taking their enemies by surprise; but always sent them fair warning when they intended to make an attack. They had now the impression that the Spaniards had left their own country because it did not furnish sufficient food for them. They therefore sent to their camp an abundant supply of poultry and corn, saying, "Eat plentifully. We disdain to attack a foe enfeebled by hunger. It would be an insult to our gods to offer them starved victims; neither do we wish to feed on emaciated bodies." We have before mentioned that it was the horrid custom of this people to offer as sacrifices to their gods prisoners taken in war, and then to banquet in savage orgies over the remains.

As Cortez moved cautiously on, adopting every precaution to guard against surprise, he suddenly emerged from a valley upon a wide-spread plain. Here he again encountered the enemy, drawn up in battle array, in numbers apparently overwhelming. It was now evening. As it was understood that the Tlascalans never attacked by night, considering it dishonorable warfare, the Spaniards pitched their tents, having posted sentinels to watch the foe with the utmost vigilance. The morning was to usher in a dreadful battle, with fearful odds against the invaders. Two chiefs who had been taken prisoners in the late battle stated that the force of the Tlascalans consisted of five divisions of ten thousand men each. Each division had its own uniform and banner, and was under the command of its appropriate chief. It was a solemn hour in the Spanish camp. "When all this was communicated to us," says Diaz, "being but mortal, and, like all others, fearing death, we prepared for battle by confessing to our reverend fathers, who were occupied during that whole night in that holy office."

Cortez released his captive chiefs, and sent them with an amicable message to their countrymen, stating that he asked only an unmolested passage through their country to Mexico, but sternly declaring, "If this proposition be refused, I will enter your capital as a conqueror. I will burn every house. I will put every inhabitant to the sword." An answer was returned of the most implacable defiance. "We will make peace," said the Tlascalans, "by devouring your bodies, and offering your hearts and your blood in sacrifice to our gods."

The morning of the 5th of September dawned cloudless and brilliant upon the two armies encamped upon the high table-lands of the Cordilleras. At an early hour the Spanish bugles roused the sleeping host. The wounded men, even, resumed their place in the ranks, so great was the peril. Cortez addressed a few inspiriting words to the troops, and placed himself at their head. Just as the sun was rising he put his army in motion. Soon they arrived in sight of the Tlascalans. The interminable host filled a vast plain, six miles square, with their thronging multitudes. The native warriors, in bands skillfully posted, were decorated with the highest appliances of barbaric pomp. As the experienced eye of Cortez ranged over their dense ranks, he estimated their numbers at more than one hundred thousand. Their weapons were slings, arrows, javelins, clubs, and rude wooden swords, sharpened with teeth of flint.

The moment the Spaniards appeared, the Tlascalans, uttering hideous yells, and filling the air with all the inconceivable clamor of their military bands, rushed upon them like the onrolling surges of the ocean. The first discharge from the native army of stones, arrows, and darts was so tremendous as to darken the sky like a thick cloud. Notwithstanding the armor worn by the Spaniards was impervious to arrow or javelin, many were wounded.

But soon the cannon was unmasked, and opened its terrific roar. Ball and grape-shot swept through the dense ranks of the natives, mowing down, in hideous mutilation, whole platoons at a discharge. The courage displayed by the Tlascalans was amazing. It has never been surpassed. Though hardly able, with their feeble weapons, to injure their adversaries, regardless of death, they filled up the gaps which the cannon opened in their ranks, and all the day long continued the unequal fight.

Immense multitudes of the dead now covered the field, and many of the chiefs were slain.

Every horse was wounded; seventy Spaniards were severely injured; one was dead, and nearly all were more or less bruised. But the artillery and the musketry were still plied with awful carnage. The commander-in-chief of the native army, finding it in vain to contend against these new and apparently unearthly weapons, at last ordered a retreat. The natives retired in as highly disciplined array as would have been displayed by French or Austrian troops. The victors, exhausted and bleeding, were glad to throw themselves upon the gory grass of the battle-field for repose. The cold wind at night, from the mountain glaciers, swept the bleak plain, and the soldiers shivered in their houseless beds. They did not sleep, however, until, in a body, they had returned thanks to the God of peace and love for their glorious victory. "It truly seemed," said Cortez, devoutly, "that God fought on our side."

It appears almost incredible that, in such a conflict, the Spanish army should have received so little injury. But Cortez made no account of any amount of loss on the part of his native allies. The Spaniards only he thought of, and they were protected with the utmost care. Their artillery and musketry kept the natives at a distance, and their helmets and coats of mail no native weapon could easily penetrate. Their danger was consequently so small that we can not give them credit for quite so much heroism as they have claimed. The enterprise, in its commencement, was bold in the extreme; but it it easy to be fearless when experience proves that there is but little peril to be encountered. They fought one hundred thousand men for a whole day, and lost *one man!*

As night enveloped in its folds the blood-stained hosts, the untiring Cortez, having buried his dead, that his loss might not be perceived by the enemy, sallied forth with the horse and a hundred foot, and four hundred of the native allies, and with fire and sword devastated six villages of a hundred houses each, taking four hundred prisoners, including men and women. Before daybreak he returned from this wild foray to the camp.

During the night the Tlascalans had been receiving re-enforcements, and when the first dawn of morning appeared, more than one hundred and forty-nine thousand natives, according to the estimate of Cortez, made a rush upon the camp. After a battle of four hours they were again compelled to retreat. "As we carried the banner of the cross," says Cortez, "and fought for our faith, God, in his glorious providence, gave us a great victory."

Night again came. Again this indomitable man of iron sinews marched forth in the darkness, with his horse, one hundred Spanish infantry, and a large party of his allies, and set three thousand houses in flames, encountering no opposition, burning out only the women and children and the unarmed inhabitants. Cortez treated all the prisoners he took very kindly, and liberated them with presents. This humanity amazed the natives, who were accustomed to a procedure so very different.

The Tlascalans were now much disheartened, and were inclined to peace. But they were quite at a loss to know how to approach the terrible foe. After much deliberation, they sent an embassage, composed of fifty of their most prominent men, bearing rich presents. Cortez suspected them of being spies. With cruelty, which will ever be an ineffaceable stigma upon his name, he ordered them all to be arrested, and their hands to be cut off. Thus awfully mutilated, these unhappy men were sent back to the Tlascalan camp with the defiant message,

"The Tlascalans may come by day or by night; the Spaniards are ready for them."

Cortez himself relates this act of atrocious cruelty. Nothing can be said in its extenuation. There was even no *proof*, but only suspicion that they were spies. It is, indeed, not at all probable that, if such were the intention, fifty of the most prominent men of the nation would have been selected. It is, however, certain, that after this all farther idea of resistance was abandoned. The commander-in-chief of the Tlascalan army, with a numerons retinue, entered the Spanish camp with proffers of submission. This brave and proud chieftain, subdued by the terrors of the resistless engines of war worked by the Spaniards, addressed Cortez in the following language, which will command universal respect and sympathy.

"I loved my country," said he, "and wished to preserve its independence. We have been beaten. I hope that you will use your victory with moderation, and not trample upon our liberties. In the name of the nation, I now tender obedience to the Spaniards. We will be as faithful in peace as we have been bold in war."

Cortez received this submission with great

secret satisfaction, for his men, worn down with fatigue, were beginning loudly to murmur. A cordial peace was soon concluded. The Tlascalans were the inveterate foes of the Mexicans, and had long been fighting against them. They yielded themselves as vassals to the King of Spain, and engaged to assist Cortez in all his enterprises. The two armies, which had recently met in such fierce and terrible encounter, now mingled together as friends and brothers. In one vast united band they marched toward the great city of Tlascala, and entered the capital in triumph.

It was, indeed, a large and magnificent city; more populous, and of more imposing architecture, Cortez asserts, than the celebrated Moorish capital, Granada, in old Spain. An immense throng flocked from the gates of the city to meet the troops. The roofs of the houses were covered with spectators. Wild music, from semi-barbarian voices and bands, filled the air. Plumed warriors hurried to and fro, and shouts of welcome seemed to rend the skies, as these hardy adventurers slowly defiled through the crowded gates and streets of the city. The police regulations were extraordinarily effective, repressing all disorder. The Spaniards were surprised to find barbers' shops, and also baths both for hot and cold water.

The submission of the Tlascalans was sincere and entire. They were convinced that the Spaniards were beings of a superior order whom it was in vain to resist. Cortez treated the vanquished natives with great courtesy and kindness. He took the Tlascalan republic under his protection, and promised to defend them from every foe.

The peril of Cortez at this juncture had been very great. The difficulty of obtaining sufficient food for his army, while ever on the march, called into requisition his utmost sagacity and exertions. No man of ordinary character could have surmounted this difficulty. Fatigue and exposure had placed many on the sick-list, and there were no hospital wagons to convey them along. Fifty-five Spaniards had died on the way. Cortez himself was seriously indisposed. Every night one half of the army kept up a vigilant watch, while all the rest slept on their arms. And Diaz records that they had no salve to dress their wounds but what was composed of the fat of the Indians whom they had slain. Whenever the enemy was defeated, he retired only to reappear in increasing numbers. Under these circumstances, it is not strange that many of the soldiers had thought of their homes, and that loud murmurs had been uttered. But this sudden peace dispelled all discontent. In the abundance and the repose of the great city of Tlascala, all past toil and hardship were forgotten.

Cortez, in his letter to the emperor, stated that so populous was Tlascala, that he presumed as many as thirty thousand persons appeared daily in the market-place of the city buying and selling. The population of the province he estimated at five hundred thousand.

CHAPTER VI.

THE MARCH TO MEXICO.

CORTEZ remained in Tlascala twenty days, to refresh his troops, and to cement his alliance with his new friends. He was all this time very diligent in making the most minute inquiries respecting the condition of the Mexican empire, and in preparing for every emergence which could arise in the continuance of his march. Bold as he was, his prudence equalled his boldness, and he left nothing willingly to the decisions of chance. The Tlascalans hated virulently their ancient foes the Mexicans, and with that fickleness of character, ever conspicuous in the uninformed multitude, became fond even to adulation of the Spaniards. With great enthusiasm they embarked in the enterprise of joining the expedition against Montezuma. All the forces of the republic were promptly raised, and placed under the command of Cortez.

Montezuma was informed of all these proceedings, and was greatly alarmed. He feared that a prophetic doom was about to descend upon him, and this apprehension wilted all his wonted energies. Thus influenced, he sent an embassy, consisting of five of the most conspicuous nobles of his empire, accompanied by a retinue of two hundred attendants, to visit the Spanish camp. Men of burden were laden down with rich presents for Cortez. The gold alone of the gifts was estimated at over fifty thousand dollars. Montezuma weakly hoped by these gifts to induce Cortez to arrest his steps. The embassadors were instructed to urge him, by all possible considerations, not to attempt to approach the Mexican capital.

Cortez returned an answer replete with expressions of Castilian courtesy, but declaring that he must obey the commands of his sovereign, which required him to visit the metropolis of the great empire.

But, in the midst of all these cares, Cortez did not forget his great mission of converting the natives to Christianity. This subject was ever prominent in his mind, and immediately upon his entrance into the city he commenced, through his interpreters, urging the chiefs to abandon their cruel idolatry. He argued with them himself, and called into requisition all the persuasive eloquence of good Father Olmedo.

The chiefs brought five maidens, all noble born, and of selected beauty. These girls were beautifully dressed, and each attended by a slave. Xicotenga, the cacique of the nation, presented his own daughter to Cortez, and requested him to assign the rest to his officers. Cortez firmly, yet courteously declined the gift, saying,

"If you wish that we should intermarry with you, you must first renounce your idolatrous worship and adore our God. He will then bless you in this life, and after death he will receive you to heaven to enjoy eternal happiness; but if you persist in the worship of your idols, which are devils, you will be drawn by them to their infernal pit, there to burn eternally in flames of fire."

He then presented to them "a beauteous image of Our Lady, with her precious Son in her arms," and attempted to explain to them the mystery of the incarnation, and the potency of the mediatorship of the Virgin.

"The God of the Christians," the Tlascalans replied, "must be great and good. We will give him a place with our gods, who are also great and good. Our god grants us victory over our enemies. Our goddess preserves us from inundations of the river. Should we forsake their worship, the most dreadful punishment would overwhelm us."

Cortez could admit of no such compromise; and he urged the destruction of the idols with so much zeal and importunity, that at last the Tlascalans became angry, and declared that on no account whatever would they abandon the gods of their fathers. Cortez now, in his turn, was roused to virtuous indignation, and he resolved that, happen what might, the true God should be honored by the swift destruction of these idols of the heathen. Encouraged by the success of his violent measures at Zempoalla, he was on the point of ordering the soldiers to make an onslaught on the gods of the Tlascalans, which would probably have so roused the warlike and exasperated natives as to have led to the entire destruction of his army in the narrow streets of the thronged capital, when the judicious and kind-hearted Father Olmedo dissuaded him from the rash enterprise. With true Christian philosophy, he plead that forced conversion was no conversion at all; that God's reign was only over willing minds and in the heart. "Religion," said this truly good man, "can not be propagated by the sword. Patient instruction must enlighten the understanding, and pious example captivate the affections, before men can be induced to abandon error and embrace the truth." It is truly refreshing to meet with these noble ideas of toleration spoken by a Spanish monk in that dark age. Let such a fact promote, not indifference to true and undefiled religion, but a generous charity.*

Cortez reluctantly yielded to these remonstrances of an ecclesiastic whose wisdom and virtue he was compelled to respect. The manifest pressure of circumstances also undoubtedly had their influence. But this ardent reformer could not yield without entering his protest.

"We can not," he said, "I admit, change the heart, but we can demolish these abominable idols, clamoring for their hecatombs of human victims, and we can introduce in their stead the blessed Virgin and her blessed child.

* "When Reverend Father Olmedo, who was a wise and good theologian, heard this, being averse to forced conversions, notwithstanding it had been done in Zempoalla, he advised Cortez to urge it no farther at present. He also observed that the destruction of their idols was a fruitless violence if the principle was not eradicated from their minds by arguments, as they would find other idols to continue their worship to elsewhere."

Will not this be a humane change? And, because we can not do the whole, shall we refuse to do a part?"

Upon one point, however, Cortez was inflexible, and to this the Tlascalans, by way of compromise, assented. He insisted that the prisons should be entirely emptied of victims destined for sacrifice. There were in the temples many poor wretches fattening for these horrid orgies. A promise was also exacted from the Tlascalans that they would hereafter desist from these heathen practices; but no sooner had the tramp of the Spaniards ceased to echo through the streets of Tlascala, than the prisons were again filled with victims, and human blood, in new torrents, crimsoned their altars.

One of the temples was also cleared out, and an altar being erected, it was converted into a Christian church. Here the young ladies destined as brides for the Spanish soldiers were baptized, their friends presenting no objections. The daughter of Xicotenga received the Christian name of Louisa. Cortez took her by the hand, and gracefully presented her to one of his captains, Alvarado, telling her father that that officer was his brother. The cacique expressed entire satisfaction at this arrangement. All were baptized and received Christian names. Many of the descendants of this beautiful and amiable Indian maiden may now be found among the grandees of Spain.

Montezuma, on the return of his embassadors, finding that no argument could dissuade Cortez, and fearing by opposition to provoke the hostility of an enemy who wielded such supernatural thunders, now decided to change his policy, and by cordiality to endeavor to win his friendship. He accordingly sent another embassy, with still richer presents, inviting Cortez to his capital, and assuring him of a warm welcome. He entreated him, however, not to enter into any alliance with the Tlascalans, the most fierce and unrelenting foes of the Mexican empire.

The time had now arrived for Cortez to resume his march. The zeal of the Tlascalans to accompany him was so great that, according to his representation, he might have taken with him one hundred thousand volunteers. He, however, considered this force too unwieldy, and accepted of but six thousand picked troops. This, however, was a strong re-enforcement, and Cortez now rode proudly at the head of a regular army which could bid defiance to all opposition.

Eighteen miles from Tlascala was situated the city of Cholula, and this city was but sixty-four miles east of the renowned Mexican metropolis. Cholula was a city whose population was estimated at one hundred thousand. As it belonged to Mexico, the bitterest animosity existed between its inhabitants and those of Tlascala. Cortez was warned by his new allies not to enter the city, as he might depend upon encountering treachery there; but the Spanish general considered himself now too strong to turn aside from any danger.

As the Spanish army approached the city, a procession came out to meet them, with banners, and bands of music, and censers smoking with incense. Numerous nobles and priests headed the procession. They received Cortez and the Zempoallans with every demonstration of friendship, but declined admitting their inveterate enemies, the Tlascalans, within their walls. Cortez accordingly ordered these allies to encamp upon the plain before the city, while he, with the rest of the army, marched with great military pomp into the metropolis, which was resounding with acclamations.

He found a beautiful city, with wide, neatly-arranged streets and handsome dwellings. It was the sacred city of the Mexicans. Many gorgeous temples lined the streets, and one of extraordinary grandeur was the most renowned sanctuary of the empire. It is alleged by some, and denied by others, that the Mexicans had invited the Spaniards into the holy city, hoping by the aid of the gods to effect their entire destruction. The Tlascalans, who were encamped outside of the city, affirmed that the women and children of the principal inhabitants were leaving the city by night. They also declared that a large body of Mexican troops were concealed near the town. Two of the Tlascalans, who had entered the city in disguise, declared that some of the streets were barricaded, and that others were undermined, and but slightly covered over, as traps for the horses. They also reported that six children had recently been sacrificed in the chief temple, which was a certain indication that some great military enterprise was on foot. Cortez, however, did not place much reliance upon this testimony from the Tlascalans. He was well aware that they would be glad, in any way, to bring down destruction on Cholula.

But more reliable testimony came from the amiable Marina. She had won the love of one of the noble ladies of the city. This woman, wishing to save Marina from destruction, informed her that a plot was in progress for the inevitable ruin of her friends. According to her account, deep pits were dug and concealed in the streets, stones carried to the tops of the houses and the temples, and that Mexican troops were secretly drawing near. The fatal hour was at hand, and escape impossible.

The energy of Cortez was now roused. Quietly he drew up the Spanish and Zempoallan troops, armed to the teeth, in the heart of the city. He sent a secret order to the Tlascalans to approach, and, at a given signal, to fall upon the surprised and unarmed Cholulans, and cut them down without mercy. He then, upon a friendly pretext, sent for the magistrates of the city and all the principal nobles. They were immediately assembled, and the signal for massacre was given.

The poor natives, taken entirely by surprise, rushed in dismay this way and that, encountering death at every corner. The Tlascalans, like hungry wolves, swept through the streets, glutting themselves with blood. It was with them the carnival of insatiable revenge. The dwellings were sacked piteously, and the city every where kindled into flame. Women and children were seized by the merciless Tlascalans to grace their triumph, and to bleed upon their altars of human sacrifice. For two days this horrid scene continued. At last, from exhaustion, the carnage ceased. The city was reduced to smouldering ruins, and pools of blood and mutilated carcases polluted the streets. The wail of the wretched survivors, homeless and friendless, rose to the ear of Heaven more dismal than the piercing shriek of anguish which is silenced by death. The argument with which Cortez defends this outrage is very laconic:

"Had I not done this to them, they would have done the same to me."

Such is war—congenial employment only for fiends. It is Satan's work, and can be efficiently prosecuted only by Satan's instruments. Six thousand Cholulans were slain in this awful massacre. The Spaniards were now sufficiently avenged. Cortez issued a proclamation offering pardon to all who had escaped the massacre, and inviting them to return to their smouldering homes. Slowly they returned, women and children, from the mountains where they had fled; some, who had feigned death,

MASSACRE IN CHOLULA.

crept from beneath the bodies of the slain, and others emerged from hiding-places in their devastated dwellings. The cacique of the Cholulans had been killed in the general slaughter. Cortez appointed a brother of the late cacique to rule over the city, and, in apparently a sincere proclamation, informed the bereaved and miserable survivors that it was with the greatest sorrow that he had found himself compelled by their treachery to this terrible punishment. The Tlascalans, glutted with the blood of their ancient foes, were compelled to surrender all their prisoners, for Cortez would allow of no human sacrifices.

Cortez thought that the natives were now in a very suitable frame of mind for his peculiar kind of conversion. They were truly very pliant. No resistance was offered to the Spanish soldiers as they tumbled the idols out of the temples, and reared in their stead the cross and the image of the Virgin. Public thanksgivings were then offered to God in the purified temples of the heathen for the victory he had vouchsafed, and mass was celebrated by the whole army.

In the year 1842, Hon. Waddy Thompson passed over the plain where once stood the city of Cholula. He thus describes it:

"The great city of Cholula was situated about six miles from the present city of Puebla. It was here the terrible slaughter was committed which has left the deepest stain upon the otherwise glorious and wonderful character of Cortez. Not a vestige—literally none—not a brick or a stone standing upon another, remains of this immense city except the great pyramid, which still stands in gloomy and solitary grandeur in the vast plain which surrounds it, and there it will stand forever. This pyramid is built of unburned bricks. Its dimensions, as given by Humboldt, are, base, 1440 feet; present height, 177; area on the summit, 45,210 square feet. A Catholic chapel now crowns the summit of this immense mound, the sides of which are covered with grass and small trees. As seen for miles along the road, an artificial mountain, standing in the solitude of a vast plain, it is a most imposing and beautiful object."

After the delay of a fortnight, Cortez resumed his march toward the capital of Mexico, which was now distant from him but twenty leagues. It was now the 29th of October. The tidings of the horrible retribution which had fallen upon Cholula spread far and wide, and it accomplished its end in preventing any farther manifestations of hostility. City after city, appalled by this exhibition of the vengeance of those foes who wielded the thunder and the lightning of heaven, and who, with the dreadful war-horse, could overtake the swiftest foe, sent in the most humble messages of submission, with accompanying presents, to propitiate the favor of the terrible invaders.

Montezuma, as he was informed of the fate of Cholula, turned pale upon his throne, and trembled in every fibre. He dreaded unspeakably to have the Spaniards enter his capital, and yet he dared not undertake to oppose them. Cortez sent embassadors before him to the capital with the following message to Montezuma:

"The Cholulans have asserted that Montezuma instigated their treachery. I will not believe it. Montezuma is a great and a powerful sovereign; he would make war in the open field, and not by cowardly stratagem. The Spaniards, however, are ready for any warfare, secret or open."

This was bold defiance. Montezuma superstitiously read in it the decree of fate announcing his doom. He returned an answer solemnly declaring that he had no part in the guilt of the Cholulans, and renewedly inviting Cortez to visit his city.

The country through which the adventurers passed became increasingly populous, luxuriant, and beautiful. They were continually met by embassies from the different cities on or near their route, endeavoring to propitiate their favor by protestations of allegiance and gifts of gold. They also perceived many indications of discontent with the reign of Montezuma, which encouraged Cortez greatly in his expectation of being able to overturn the empire, by availing himself of the alienation existing in its constituent parts. Multitudes of the disaffected joined the army of Cortez, where they were all warmly welcomed. "Thus," says Clavigero, "the farther the Spaniards advanced into the country, the more they continued to increase their forces; like a rivulet which, by the accession of other streams, swells in its course into a large river."

For several days they toiled resolutely along, "recommending," says Diaz, "our souls to the Lord Jesus Christ, who had brought us through our past dangers," until, from the heights of Ithualco, they looked down over the majestic, the enchanting valley of Mexico. A more per-

FIRST VIEW OF THE MEXICAN CAPITAL

fectly lovely scene has rarely greeted human eyes. In the far distance could be discerned, through the transparent atmosphere, the dim blue outline of the mountains by which the almost boundless basin of Mexico was girdled. Forests and rivers, orchards and lakes, cultivated fields and beautiful villages adorned the landscape. The magnificent city of Mexico was situated, in queenly splendor, upon islands in the bosom of a series of lakes more than a hundred miles in length. Innumerable towns, with their lofty temples, and white, picturesque dwellings, fringed the margin of the crystal waters. The circumference of the valley girdled by the mountains was nearly two hundred miles.

The Spaniards gazed upon the enchanting scene with amazement, and many of them with alarm. They saw indications of civilization and of power far beyond what they had anticipated. Cortez, however, relying upon the efficiency of gunpowder, and also deeming himself invincible while the sacred banner of the cross waved over his army, marched boldly on. The love of plunder was a latent motive omnipotent in his soul, and he saw undreamed of wealth lavishly spread before him. Though Cortez was, at this period of his life, a stranger to the sordid vice of avarice, he coveted intensely boundless wealth, to be profusely distributed in advancing his great plans.*

Montezuma was continually vacillating as to the course to be pursued. At one hour he would resolve to marshal his armies, and fall, if fall he must, gloriously, amid the ruins of his empire. The next hour timidity would be in the ascendant, and a new embassy would be sent to Cortez, with courteous speeches and costly

* Hon. Waddy Thompson thus describes the appearance of the great valley of Mexico at the present time. "The road passes within about twenty miles of the mountain of Pococatapetl, the highest point of the territory of Mexico; but the brightness of the atmosphere, and a tropical sun shining upon the snow with which it is always covered, makes the distance seem very much shorter—not, indeed, more than one or two miles. In descending the mountain, at about the distance of twenty-five miles the first glimpse is caught of the city and valley of Mexico. No description can convey to the reader any adequate idea of the effect upon one who, for the first time, beholds that magnificent prospect. With what feelings must Cortez have regarded it when he first saw it from the top of the mountain between the snow-covered volcanoes of Pococatapetl and Iztaccihuatl, a short distance to the left of where the road now runs! The valley was not then, as it is now, for the greater part a barren waste, but was studded all over with the homes of men, containing more than forty cities, besides towns and villages without number. Never has such a vision burst upon the eyes of mortal man since that upon which the seer of old looked down from Pisgah."

gifts. The unhappy monarch, in his despair, had gone to one of the most sacred of the sanctuaries of the empire to mourn and to pray. Here he passed eight days in the performance of all the humiliating and penitential rites of his religion. But each day Cortez drew nearer, and the crowds accumulating around him increased.

The spirit of Montezuma was now so crushed that he sent an embassy to Cortez offering him four loads of gold for himself, and one for each of his captains, and he also promised to pay a yearly tribute to the King of Spain, if the dreaded conqueror would turn back. This messenger met the Spanish army upon the heights of Ithualco, as they were gazing with admiration upon the goodly land spread out before them. Cortez listened with much secret satisfaction to this messenger, as an indication of the weakness and the fear of the great monarch. Returning the laconic answer, "I must see Montezuma, and deliver to him personally the message of the emperor my master," he more eagerly pressed on his way.

Montezuma received this response as the doom decreed to him by fate. "Of what avail," the unhappy monarch is reported to have said, "is resistance, when the gods have declared themselves against us? Yet I mourn most for the old and infirm, the women and children, too feeble to fight or to fly. For myself and the brave men around me, we must bare our breasts to the storm, and meet it as we may."

The Spaniards had now arrived at the city of Amaquemecan. They were received by the principal inhabitants of the place with an ostentatious display of courtesy and friendship. Two very large stone buildings were provided for their accommodation. This profuse hospitality was excited by terror. After resting here two days, Cortez resumed his march. Their path still led through smiling villages and fields of maize, and through gardens blooming with gorgeous flowers, which the natives cultivated with religious and almost passionate devotion.

At last they arrived at Ayotzingo—the Venice of the New World—an important town, built on wooden piles in the waters of Lake Chalco. Gondolas of every variety of color, and of graceful structure, glided through the liquid streets. The main body of the Spanish army encamped outside of the city. A vast concourse of the natives flocked to the camp. Cortez became suspicious of premeditated treachery, and fifteen or twenty of the natives were heartlessly shot down, as an intimidation. The terrified Indians did not venture to resent this cruel requital of their hospitality.

After remaining here two days, the march was again resumed along the southern shores of Lake Chalco. Clusters of villages, embowered in luxuriant foliage, and crimson with flowers, fringed the lake. The waters were covered with the light boats of the natives, gliding in every direction. At last they came to a narrow dike or causeway, five miles long, and so narrow that but two or three horsemen could ride abreast. In the middle of this causeway, which separated Lake Chalco from Lake Xochicalco, was built the town of Cuitlahuac, which Cortez described as the most beautiful he had yet seen. Before the mansions of the principal inhabitants there were lawns ornamented with trees and shrubbery. Temples and lofty towers rose in much majesty of architecture. Floating gardens were constructed on the lake, and innumerable boats, plied by the strong arms of the native rowers, almost covered the placid waters. As the Spaniards marched along this narrow causeway, the crowd became so immense that Cortez was obliged to resort to threats of violence to force his way. The place was so very favorable for the natives to make an assault, that Cortez conducted the march with the utmost possible vigilance, and commanded the Indians not to come near his ranks unless they chose to be regarded as enemies. The adventurers were, however, received in Cuitlahuac with the utmost kindness, and all their wants were abundantly supplied.

When they had crossed the narrow causeway, and had arrived on the other side of the lake, they entered the city of Iztapalapan, which contained, according to their estimate, about fifteen thousand houses. The city was in the near vicinity of the capital. The natives, with refinement and taste not yet equaled by the money-making millions of North America, had allotted land in the centre of the city for a vast public garden, blooming with flowers of every variety of splendor. A large aviary was filled with birds of gorgeous plumage and sweet song. A stone reservoir, of ample dimensions, contained water to irrigate the grounds, and it was also abundantly stored with fish. Many of the chiefs of the neighboring cities had assembled here to meet Cortez. They received him with courtesy, with hospitality, but with reserve. He was now but a few miles from the renowned metropolis of Montezuma, and the turrets of the lofty temples of idolatry which embellished the capital glittered in the sunlight before him.

Another night passed away, and, as another morning dawned, the Spanish army was again on the march. It was the 8th of November, 1519. When they drew near the city, they were first met by a procession of a thousand of the principal inhabitants, adorned with waving plumes, and clad in finely-embroidered mantles. They announced that their renowned Emperor Montezuma was advancing to welcome the strangers. They were now upon the causeway which led from the main land to the island city. The long and narrow way was thronged with crowds which could not be numbered, while on each side the lake was darkened with boats. Soon the glittering train of the emperor appeared in the distance.

Montezuma was accompanied by the highest possible pomp of semi-barbarian etiquette and splendor. He was seated in a gorgeous palanquin, waving with plumes and glittering with gold, and was borne on the shoulders of four noblemen. Three officers, each holding a golden rod, walked before him. Others supported over his head, by four posts, to shelter him from the sun, a canopy of beautiful workmanship, richly embellished with green feathers, and gold, and precious gems. The monarch wore upon his head a golden crown, surmounted by a rich head-dress of plumes. A mantle, richly embroidered with the most costly ornaments, was folded gracefully upon his shoulders. Buskins, fringed with gold, fitted closely to his legs, and the soles of his shoes were of gold. He was tall, well formed, and a peculiarly handsome man.

As the monarch drew near, Cortez dismounted, and advanced on foot to meet him. At the same time Montezuma alighted from his palanquin, and, leaning upon the arms of two of the highest members of his court, with great dignity approached his dreaded guest. His attendants in the mean time spread before their monarch rich carpets, that his sacred feet might not come in contact with the ground. An expression of anxiety and of deep melancholy overspread the countenance of the sovereign.

The Mexican emperor and the Spanish marauder met in the interchange of all Mexican and Castilian courtesies. After the exchange of a few words, the whole blended cortège march-

THE MEETING OF CORTEZ AND MONTEZUMA.

ed through the immense crowd, which opened before them, and entered the imperial city. "Who," exclaims Diaz, "could count the number of men, women, and children which thronged the streets, the canals, and terraces on the tops of the houses on that day? The whole of what I saw on this occasion is so strongly imprinted on my memory that it appears to me as if it had happened only yesterday. Glory to our Lord Jesus Christ, who gave us courage to venture upon such dangers, and brought us safely through them."

Montezuma himself conducted Cortez to the quarters which he had prepared for his reception in the heart of the metropolis. With refinement of politeness which would have done honor to the court of Louis XIV., he said, on retiring,

"You are now, with your brothers, in your own house. Refresh yourselves after your fatigue, and be happy until I return."

The spot assigned to the Spaniards was an immense palace, or, rather, range of mansions, in the very centre of the metropolis, erected by the father of Montezuma. The buildings inclosed an immense court-yard. The whole was surrounded by a strong stone wall, surmounted with towers for defense and ornament. Cortez could not have constructed for himself a more admirable citadel for the accomplishment of his ambitious and violent purposes. The apartment assigned to the Spanish chieftain was tapestried with the finest embroidered cotton. The rooms and courts were so large as to afford ample accommodations for the whole Spanish army.

"This edifice was so large," writes one of the historians of that day, "that both the Spaniards and their allies, who, together with the women and the servants whom they brought with them, exceeded seven thousand in number, were lodged in it. Every where there was the greatest cleanliness and neatness. Almost all the chambers had beds of mats, of rushes, and of palm, according to the custom of the people, and other mats, in a round form, for pillows. They had coverlets of fine cotton, and chairs made of single pieces of wood. Some of the chambers were also carpeted with mats, and the walls were hung with tapestry beautifully colored."

Cortez, with vigilance which never slept, immediately fortified his quarters, so as to guard against any possible surprise. Artillery was planted to sweep every avenue. Sentinels were posted at important points, with orders to observe the same diligence by night and by day as if they were in the midst of hostile armies. A large division of the troops was always on guard, prepared for every possible emergency.

In the evening, Montezuma returned, with great pomp, to visit his terrible guests, and to inquire if they were provided with every thing which could promote their comfort. He brought with him presents of great value for Cortez and his officers, and also for each one of the privates in the Spanish camp. A long conference ensued, during which Montezuma betrayed his apprehension that the Spaniards were the conquerors indicated by tradition and prophecy as decreed to overthrow the Mexican power. Cortez artfully endeavored to frame his reply so as to encourage this illusion. He expatiated at great length upon the wealth and the resistless power of the emperor whom he served. "My master wishes," said he, "to alter certain laws and customs in this kingdom, and particularly to present to you a religion far superior to the bloody creed of Mexico." He then, with great earnestness, unfolded to the respectful monarch the principal doctrines of Christianity—the one living and true God—the advent of the Savior, his atonement, and salvation through faith in him—the rites of baptism and of the Lord's Supper—the eternal rewards of the righteous, and the unending woes of the wicked. To these remarks Cortez added an indignant remonstrance against the abomination of human sacrifices, and of eating the flesh of the wretched victims. By way of application to this sermon, which was truthful in its main sentiments, and unquestionably sincere, this most singular of missionaries called out the artillery. We would not speak lightly of sacred things in stating the fact that Cortez considered gunpowder as one of the most important of the means of grace. He judged that the thunder of his cannon, reverberating through the streets of the astounded capital, would exert a salutary influence upon the minds of the natives, and produce that pliancy of spirit, that child-like humility, so essential both to voluntary and involuntary conversion. The most important truth and the most revolting falsehood here bewilderingly meet and blend.

The sun had now gone down, and the short twilight was fading away into the darkness of the night, when, at a given signal, every cannon was discharged. The awful roar rolled through the streets of the metropolis, and froze the hearts of the people with terror. Were these strange beings, they inquired among themselves, who thus wielded the heaviest thunders of heaven, gods or demons? Volley after volley, in appalling peals, burst from the city, and resounded over the silent lake. Dense volumes of suffocating smoke, scarcely moved by the tranquil air, settled down upon the streets. Silence ensued. The voice of Cortez had been heard in tones never to be forgotten. The stars came out in the serene sky, and a brilliant tropical night enveloped in its folds the fearless Spaniard and the trembling Mexican.

It was the night of the 8th of November. But seven months had elapsed since the Spaniards landed in the country. The whole Spanish force, exclusive of the natives whom they had induced to join them, consisted of but four hundred and fifty men. They were now two hundred miles from the coast, in the very heart of an empire numbering many millions, and by sagacity, courage, and cruelty, they had succeeded in bringing both monarch and people into almost entire submission to their sway. The genius of romance can narrate few tales more marvelous.

CHAPTER VII.

THE METROPOLIS INVADED.

THE next morning, Cortez, with a showy retinue of horsemen, prancing through streets upon which hoof had never before trodden, called upon the emperor. The streets were lined, and the roofs of the houses crowded with multitudes gazing upon the amazing spectacle. The Spanish chieftain was kindly received by the emperor, and three days were appointed to introduce him to all the objects of interest in the capital. Tenochtitlan was the native name by which the imperial city was then known.

They first visited the great public square or market-place. An immense concourse was here assembled, engaged in peaceful traffic. Three judges sat in state at the end of the square, to settle all difficulties. A numerous body of police, ever moving through the crowd, prevented all riot or confusion. Though there were many other minor market-places scattered through the city, this was the principal one.

Cortez then expressed the wish that he might be conducted to the great pyramidal temple, which reared its lofty structure from the heart of the city. The summit of the pyramid was an extended plain, where several hundred priests could officiate in sacrifice. The corners of the area were ornamented with towers. One hundred and fourteen steps led to the summit of the temple. Several large altars stood here, besmeared with the blood of human sacrifices, and there was also a hideous image of a dragon polluted with gore.

From this towering eminence the whole adjacent country lay spread out before the eye of Cortez in surpassing loveliness. Gardens, groves, villages, waving fields of grain, and the wide expanse of the placid lakes, covered with boats gliding rapidly over the mirrored waters, presented a scene of beauty which excited the enthusiasm of Cortez to the highest pitch. They then entered the sanctuaries of the temple, where human hearts were smoking, and almost throbbing, upon the altars before the revolting images of their gods. On the summit of the temple there was an enormous drum or gong, which was struck when the miserable victim was shrieking beneath the knife of sacrifice. Its doleful tones, it was said, floating over the still waters of the lake, could be heard at the distance of many miles.

From these sickening scenes Cortez turned away in disgust, and exclaimed indignantly to Montezuma,

"How can you, wise and powerful as you are, put trust in such representatives of the devil? Why do you allow your people to be butchered before these abominable idols? Let me place here the cross, and the image of the blessed Virgin and of her Son, and the influence of these detestable idols will soon vanish."

Montezuma, shocked by words which he deemed so blasphemous, and dreading the swift vengeance of the gods, hurried his irreverent guest away.

"Go," said he, "go hence, I entreat you, while I remain to appease, if possible, the wrath of the gods whom you have so dreadfully provoked."

But these scenes aroused anew the religious zeal of Cortez and his companions. As they returned to their lodgings, they immediately converted one of the halls of their residence into a Christian chapel. Here the rites of the Roman Catholic Church were introduced, and the whole army of Cortez, with soldierly devotion, attended mass every day. Good Father Olmedo, with perhaps a clouded intellect, but with that recognition of the universal brotherhood of man which sincere piety ever confers, prayed fervently for God's blessing upon his frail children of every name and nation.

The Spaniards estimated the population of the city at about five hundred thousand. The streets were very regularly laid out at right angles. Many of them were wide, and lined with shade-trees. The houses of the common people were small but comfortable cottages, built of reeds or of bricks baked in the sun. The dwellings of the nobles and of the more wealthy inhabitants were strongly-built mansions of stone, very extensive on the ground floor, though generally but one story high. They were inclosed in gardens blooming with flowers. Fountains of cool water, conveyed through earthen pipes, played in the court-yards. The police regulations were unsurpassed by those of any city in Europe. A thousand persons were continually employed in sweeping and watering the streets. So clean were the well-cemented pavements kept, that "a man could walk through the streets," says one of the Spanish historians, "with as little danger of soiling his feet as his hands."

Day after day was passed in the interchange of visits, and in the careful examination by Cortez of the strength and the resources of the city. He had now been a week in the capital, and the question naturally arose, What is next to be done? He was, indeed, perplexed to decide this question. Montezuma treated him with such extraordinary hospitality, supplying all his wants, and leaving him at perfect liberty, that it was difficult for one, who laid any claim whatever to a conscience, to find occasion to pick a quarrel. To remain inactive, merely enjoying the luxury of a most hospitable entertainment, was not only accomplishing nothing, but was also enervating the army. It was also to be apprehended that the Mexicans would gradually regain their courage as they counted the small number of the invaders, and fall upon them with resistless power.

The Tlascalans, who had rioted in blood at Cholula, seemed anxious for a renewal of that scene of awful butchery in the streets of Mexico. They assured Cortez that he had every thing to fear from the treachery of Montezuma; that he had lured them into the city but to in-close them in a trap; that the drawbridges of the causeways need but be removed, and escape for the Spaniards would be impossible. They assured him that the Mexican priests had counseled Montezuma, in the name of the gods, to admit the strangers into the capital that he might cut them off at a blow. It was obvious, even to the meanest soldier, that all this might be true, and that they were in reality in a trap from which it would be exceedingly difficult to extricate themselves, should the Mexicans manifest any resolute hostility.

On the east the island city had no connection with the main land, and could only be approached over the broad waters of the lake by canoes. On the west the city was entered by an artificial causeway, built of earth and stone, a mile and a half in length, and but thirty feet in breadth. A similar causeway on the northwest, three miles long, connected the city with the main land. There was another causeway on the south, six miles long. There were many openings along these causeways, through which the waters of the lake flowed unimpeded. These openings were bridged over by means of timber. The destruction of these bridges, which might be accomplished at any hour, would render an escape for the Spaniards almost impossible.

CITY OF MEXICO.

In this dilemma, the bold Spaniard adopted the audacious yet characteristic plan of seizing Montezuma, who was regarded with almost religious adoration by his subjects, and holding him as a hostage. The following occurrence furnished Cortez with a plausible pretext to pick a quarrel.

We have before mentioned that the Totonacs,

wishing to escape from the subjection of the Mexicans, had acknowledged themselves vassals of the King of Spain. When the officers of Montezuma attempted, as usual, to collect the taxes, the Totonacs refused payment. Force was resorted to, and a conflict arose. The colony at Vera Cruz immediately sent some soldiers to aid their allies, headed by Escalente, the commander of the Spanish garrison. In the engagement which ensued, Escalente and seven of his men were mortally wounded, one horse was killed, and one Spaniard taken captive, who soon, however, died of his wounds. Still the Spaniards, with their Totonac allies, were victorious, and repelled the Mexicans with much slaughter. The vanquished party cut off the head of their unfortunate prisoner, and carried it in triumph to several cities, to show that their foes were not invulnerable.

With alacrity Cortez availed himself of this event. He immediately repaired to the palace of Montezuma, and, with bitter reproaches, accused him of treacherously ordering an assault upon the Spaniards who had been left at Vera Cruz. Sternly the pitiless Spaniard demanded reparation for the loss, and atonement for the insult. Montezuma, confounded at this unexpected accusation, earnestly declared that the order had not been issued by him, but that the distant officer had acted on his own responsibility, without consulting the sovereign. Ungenerously he added that, in proof of his innocence, he would immediately command the offending officer, Qualpopoca, and his accomplices, to be brought prisoners to Mexico, and to be delivered to Cortez for any punishment which the Spaniards might decree.

Cortez now feigned a relenting mood, and declared that he could not himself doubt the word of the emperor, but that something more was requisite to appease the rage of his followers. "Nothing," said he, "can satisfy them of your sincerity and of your honorable intentions, unless you will leave your palace, and take up your abode in the Spanish quarters. This will pacify my men, and they will honor you there as becomes a great monarch."

When Marina interpreted this strange proposal, Montezuma was for a moment so struck with amazement as to be almost bereft of speech. His cheek was flushed with shame and rage, and then the hectic glow passed away into deadly paleness. His ancient spirit was for a moment revived, and he exclaimed, indignantly,

"When did ever a monarch suffer himself to be tamely led to a prison? Even were I willing to debase myself in so vile a manner, would not my people immediately arm themselves to set me free?"

One of the impetuous attendants of Cortez, as the altercation continued, exclaimed, grasping his sword,

"Why waste time in vain? Let us either seize him instantly or stab him to the heart."

Montezuma, though he did not understand his words, observed the threatening voice and the fierce gesture, and, turning to the amiable interpretress, Marina, inquired what he said.

"Sire," she replied, with her characteristic mildness and tact, "as your subject, I desire your happiness; but as the confidante of those men, I know their secrets, and am acquainted with their character. If you yield to their wishes, you will be treated with all the honor due to your royal person; but if you persist in your refusal, your life will be in danger."

Montezuma, reading in these events, as he supposed, but the decrees of fate, now yielded. He called his officers, and informed them of his decision. Though they were plunged into utter consternation by the intelligence, they did not venture to question his will. The imperial palanquin was brought, and the humiliated emperor was conveyed, followed by a mourning crowd, to the Spanish quarters. Montezuma endeavored to appease them, and to prevent any act of violence, by assuring the people that it was his own pleasure to go and reside with his friends. He was now so thoroughly convinced of the resistless power of the Spaniards, and that he was swept along by the decrees of fate, that he dreaded any movement of resistance on the part of his people.*

He was magnificently imprisoned. His own servants were permitted to attend him, and he continued to administer the government as if he had been in his own palace. All the forms of courtly etiquette were scrupulously observed in approaching his person. Ostensibly to confer upon him greater honor, a body-guard of stern Spanish veterans was appointed for his protection. This body-guard, with all external demonstrations of obsequiousness, watched him by night and by day, rendering escape impossible.

* Bernal Diaz says, "It having been decided that we should seize the person of the king, we passed the whole of the preceding night in praying to our Lord that he would be pleased to guide us, so that what we were going to do should redound to his holy service."

This violence, however, was but the beginning of the humiliation and anguish imposed upon the unhappy monarch. The governor, Qualpopoca, who had ventured to resist the Spaniards, was brought a captive to the capital, with his son and fifteen of the principal officers who had served under him. They were immediately surrendered to Cortez, that he might determine their crime and their punishment. Qualpopoca was put to the torture. He avowed, in his intolerable agony, that he had only obeyed the orders of his sovereign. Cortez, who wished to impress the Mexicans with the idea that it was the greatest of all conceivable crimes to cause the death of a Spaniard, determined to inflict upon them a punishment which should appal every beholder. They were all doomed to be burned alive in the great market-place of the city. To allow no time for any resistance to be organized, they were immediately led out for execution. In the royal arsenals there was an immense amount of arrows, spears, javelins, and other wooden martial weapons, which had been collected for the defense of the city. These the soldiers gathered, thus disarming the population, and heaped them up in an immense funeral pile.

While these atrocities were in preparation, Cortez entered the presence of his captive, Montezuma, and sternly accused him of being an accomplice in the death of the Spaniards. He then pitilessly ordered the soldiers who accompanied him to bind upon the hands and the feet of the monarch the iron manacles of a felon. It was one of the most cruel insults which could have been inflicted upon fallen majesty. Montezuma was speechless with horror, and his attendants, who regarded the person of their sovereign with religious veneration, wailed and wept. The shackles being adjusted, Cortez turned abruptly upon his heel, leaving the monarch in the endurance of this ignominious punishment, and went out to attend to the execution of the victims, who were already bound to the stake.

The cruel fires were then kindled. The flames crackled, and rose in fierce, devouring billows around the sufferers. The stern soldiery stood, with musketry and artillery loaded and primed, ready to repel any attempts at rescue. Thousands of Mexicans, with no time for consideration, gazed with awe upon the appalling spectacle ; and the Indian chieftains, without a struggle or an audible groan, were burned to ashes. The dreadful execution being terminated, and the blood of the Spaniards being thus avenged by the degradation of the sovereign and the death of his officers, Cortez returned to Montezuma, and ordered the fetters to be struck from his limbs.

Step after step of violence succeeded, until Montezuma was humbled to the dust. The fearful rigor with which Cortez had punished even the slightest attempt to resist the Spaniards overawed the nation. Cortez was now virtually the Emperor of Mexico. The general laws and customs of the nation remained unchanged; but Cortez issued his commands through Montezuma, and the mandates of the imprisoned sovereign were submissively obeyed. With great skill, the Spanish adventurer availed himself of these new powers. He sent a Spanish commission, by the authority and under the protection of Montezuma, to explore the empire—to ascertain its strength and its weakness, its wealth and its resources. These officers went to nearly all the provinces, and, by their arrogant display of power, endeavored to intimidate the natives, and to prepare them for entire subjection to Spain.

Mexican officers, whose fidelity Cortez suspected, were degraded, and their places supplied by others whose influence he had secured. A general contribution of gold was exacted throughout the whole Mexican territories for the benefit of the conquerors.

A large sum was thus collected. One fifth of this was laid aside for his majesty, the King of Spain. Another fifth was claimed by Cortez. The remaining portion was so greatly absorbed to defray the innumerable expenses of the expedition, that only about one hundred crowns fell to the lot of each soldier. This excited discontent so deep and loud that Cortez was compelled to attempt to pacify his men by a public address.

"He called us together," says Diaz, "and in a long set speech, gave us a great many honeyed words, which he had an extraordinary facility of doing, wondering how we could be so solicitous about a little paltry gold when the whole country would soon be ours, with all its rich mines, wherewith there was enough to make us great lords and princes, and I know not what."

Cortez was cautious as well as bold. To prepare for a retreat in case of necessity, should the Mexicans seize their arms and break down their bridges, he wished, without exciting the suspicions of the natives, to build some vessels which would command the lake. He accomplished this with his usual address. In conversation with Montezuma, he gave the monarch such glowing accounts of floating palaces, which would glide rapidly over the water without oars, as to excite the intense curiosity of his captive. Montezuma expressed a strong desire to see these wonderful fabrics. Cortez, under the pretext of gratifying this desire, very obligingly consented to build two brigantines. The resources of the empire were immediately placed at the disposal of Cortez. A multitude of men were sent to the forest to cut down ship-timber and draw it to the lake. Several hundred *men of burden* were dispatched to Vera Cruz to transport naval stores from that place to Mexico. Aided by so many strong arms, the Spanish carpenters soon succeeded in constructing two vessels, which amused the monarch and his people, and which afforded the Spaniards an invaluable resource in the hour of danger.

But the insolent bearing of the Spaniards had now become to many quite unendurable. Cacamatzin, the chief of the powerful city of Tezcuco, at the farther extremity of the lake, was a nephew of Montezuma. He was a bold man, and his indignation, in view of the pusillanimity of his uncle, at last overleaped his prudence. He began to assemble an army to make war upon the Spaniards. The Mexicans began to rally around their new leader. The indications were alarming to Cortez, and even Montezuma became apprehensive that he might lose his crown, for it was reported that Cacamatzin, regarding his uncle as degraded and a captive, intended to seize the reins of empire. Under these circumstances, Cortez and Montezuma acted in perfect harmony against their common foe. After several unsuccessful stratagems to get possession of the person of the bold chieftain, Montezuma sent some of his nobles, who secretly seized him, and brought him a prisoner to the capital, where he was thrust into prison. A partisan of Cortez was sent to take the place of Cacamatzin as governor of the province of Tezcuco. Thus this danger was averted.

Cortez still felt much solicitude concerning the judgment of the King of Spain respecting his bold assumption of authority. He well knew that Velasquez, the governor of Cuba, whose dominion he had so recklessly renounced, would report the proceedings to the court at Madrid, sustained by all the influence he could command. To conciliate his sovereign, and to bribe him to indulgence, he extorted from the weeping, spirit-crushed sovereign of Mexico an acknowledgment of vassalage to the King of Spain. This humiliating deed was invested with much imposing pomp. All the nobles and lords were assembled in a large hall in the Spanish quarters. The poor monarch wept bitterly, and his voice often broke with emotion as he tremblingly said,

"I speak as the gods direct. Our prophets have told us that a new race is to come to supplant our own. The hour has arrived. The sceptre passes from my hands by the decrees of fate which no one can resist. I now surrender to the King of the East my power and allegiance, and promise to pay to him an annual tribute."

A general outburst of amazement and indignation from the nobles followed this address. Cortez, apprehensive that he might have proceeded a little too far, endeavored to appease the rising agitation by the assurance that his master had no intention to deprive Montezuma of his regal power, or to make any innovations upon the manners and the laws of the Mexicans. The act of submission and homage was, however, executed with all the formalities which Cortez saw fit to prescribe. The nobles retired, exasperated to the highest degree, and burning with desires for vengeance.

Encouraged by these wonderful successes, and by the tame submission of the monarch, Cortez resolved upon the entire overthrow, by violence if necessary, of the whole system of idolatry, and to introduce Catholic Christianity in its stead. He had often, with the most importunate zeal, urged Montezuma to renounce his false gods and to embrace the Christian faith. But superstition was too firmly enthroned in the heart of the Mexican monarch to be easily supplanted. To every thing but this the monarch was ready to yield; but every proposition to renounce his gods he rejected with horror. Cortez at length firmly ordered his soldiers to march to the temples and sweep them clean of every vestige of paganism. This roused the priests. They seized their arms, and the alarm was spread rapidly through the streets of the city. Vast multitudes, grasping such weapons as they could get, assembled around the temples, resolved to brave every peril in defense of their religion. Matters assumed an aspect so threatening, that, for the first time, Cortez found it necessary to draw back. He contented himself with simply ejecting the gods from one of the shrines, and in erecting in their stead an image of the Virgin.

There were now many indications of approaching trouble. The natives were greatly provoked, and it was evident that they were watching for a favorable opportunity to rise against their invaders. Cortez practiced the most sleepless vigilance. Diaz speaks thus of the hardships he and his comrades endured:

"During the nine months that we remained in Mexico, every man, without any distinction between officers and soldiers, slept on his arms, in his quilted jacket and gorget. They lay on mats or straw spread on the floor, and each was obliged to hold himself as alert as if he had been on guard. This became so habitual to me, that even now, in my advanced age, I always sleep in my clothes, and never in any bed."

Just in this crisis alarming intelligence was received from the commander of the garrison at Vera Cruz. One of the ships of the delegation sent to Spain, of which we have previously spoken, had, contrary to the orders of Cortez, stopped at Cuba. In this way the indignant governor, Velasquez, learned that Cortez had renounced all connection with him, and had set up an independent colony. His anger was roused to the utmost, and he resolved upon summary vengeance. It so happened that Velasquez had just received from his sovereign the appointment of governor *for life*, and was authorized to prosecute discoveries in Mexico with very extensive and exclusive privileges and powers.

He immediately fitted out an armament consisting of nineteen ships, with eighty horsemen, fourteen hundred soldiers, and twenty pieces of cannon. This was, in that day, a formidable force. The commandant, Narvaez, was ordered to seize Cortez and his principal officers, and send them in chains to Cuba. He was then, in the name of Velasquez, to prosecute the discovery and the conquest of the country.

After a prosperous voyage, the fleet cast anchor in the Bay of St. Juan de Ulua, and the soldiers were landed. Narvaez then sent a summons to the governor of Vera Cruz to surrender. Sandoval, the commandant, however, being zealously attached to Cortez, seized the envoy and his attendants, and sent them in chains to the capital, with intelligence of the impending peril. Cortez, with his wonted sagacity, received them as friends, ordered their chains to be struck off, condemned the severity of Sandoval, and loaded them with caresses and presents. He thus won their confidence, and drew from them all the particulars of the force, and the intentions of the expedition. Cortez had great cause for alarm when he learned that Narvaez was instructed to espouse the cause of Montezuma; to assure the Mexican monarch that the violence which he had suffered was unauthorized by the King of Spain, and that he was ready to assist Montezuma and his subjects in repelling the invaders from the capital. From peril so imminent no ordinary man could have extricated himself. Narvaez was already on the march, and the natives, enraged against Cortez, were in great numbers joining the standard of the new-comers. Already emissaries from the camp of Narvaez had reached the capital, and had communicated to Montezuma, through the nobles, intelligence that Narvaez was marching to his relief. Montezuma was overjoyed, and his nobles were elated with hope, as they secretly collected arms and marshaled their forces for battle.

Cortez immediately dispatched Father Olmedo to meet Narvaez to propose terms of accommodation. He was fully aware that no such terms as he proposed could be acceded to; but Olmedo and his attendants were enjoined, as the main but secret object of their mission, to do every thing they could, by presents, caresses, promises, and glowing descriptions of the greatness of Cortez, his power, and the glory opening before him, to induce the officers and soldiers of Narvaez to abandon his standard, and range themselves under the banner of Cortez.

At the same time, Cortez, leaving one hundred and fifty men, under Alvarado, to guard the fortified camp in the metropolis, set out by forced marches, with the rest of his force, to fall unexpectedly upon Narvaez. His strength did not exceed two hundred and fifty men. In a great emergency like this, the natives could not be trusted. As Cortez drew near his foe, he found that Narvaez was encamped upon a great plain in the vicinity of Zempoalla. A terrible tempest arose. Black clouds darkened the sky, and the rain fell in floods. The soldiers of Narvaez, drenched through and through by the unceasing torrents, demanded to be led to the shelter of the houses in Zempoalla. They deemed it impossible that any foe could approach in such a storm; but the storm, in all its pitiless fury, was the very re-enforcement which Cortez and his men desired. Black midnight came, and the careering tempest swept the deluged streets of Zempoalla, driving even the sentinels to seek shelter.

Cortez gathered his little band around him, and roused them, by a vigorous harangue, for an immediate attack. The odds were fearful. Cortez had but two hundred and fifty men. Narvaez had fifteen hundred, with nineteen pieces of artillery and eighty horsemen. Giving the soldiers for their countersign the inspiring words, "The Holy Spirit," they rushed through the darkness and the raging storm upon the unsuspecting foe. They first directed their energies for the capture of the artillery. The party who made this attack was headed by Pizarro, "an active lad," says Diaz, "whose name, however, was at that time as little known as that of Peru." The guns were seized, after a short and not a very sanguinary struggle. They then, without a moment's delay, turned upon the horsemen. But the sleeping foe was now effectually aroused. A short scene of consternation, clamor, horror, and blood ensued. The companions of Cortez fought with the energies of despair. To them, defeat was certain death. The soldiers of Narvaez were bewildered. Many of them, even before the battle, were half disposed to abandon Narvaez and join the standard of Cortez, of whose renown they had heard such glowing accounts. Taken by a midnight surprise, they fought manfully for a time. But at length, in the hot and tumultuary fight, a spear pierced the cheek of Narvaez, and tore out one of his eyes. He was struck down and made a prisoner. This led to an immediate surrender. The genius of Cortez had most signally triumphed. Though many were wounded in this conflict, but two men on the side of Cortez were killed, and fifteen of the party of Narvaez.

The artful conqueror loaded the vanquished with favors, and soon succeeded in winning nearly all of them to engage in his service. With enthusiasm these new recruits, thus singularly gained, rallied around him, eager to march in the paths of glory to which such a leader could guide them.

This achievement was hardly accomplished ere a new peril menaced the victorious Spaniard. An express arrived from the Mexican metropolis with the intelligence that the Mexicans had risen in arms; that they had attacked the Spaniards in their quarters, and had killed several, and had wounded more; that they had also seized the two brigantines, destroyed the magazine of provisions, and that the whole garrison was in imminent danger of destruction.

Immediately collecting his whole force, now greatly augmented by the accession of the vanquished troops of Narvaez, with their cavalry and artillery, Cortez hastened back from Zempoalla to the rescue of his beleaguered camp. His army now, with his strangely acquired re-enforcement, amounted to over a thousand infantry and a hundred cavalry, besides several thousands of the natives, whom he recruited from his allies, the Totonacs.

The danger was so imminent that his troops were urged to the utmost possible rapidity of march. At Tlascala, two thousand of those fierce warriors joined him; but as he advanced into the territory of Montezuma, he met every where the evidences of strong disaffection to his cause. The nobles avoided his camp. The inhabitants of cities and villages retired at his approach. No food was brought to him. The natives made no attempt to oppose a force so resistless, but they left before him a path of silence and solitude.

When the Spaniards arrived at the causeway which led to the city, they found, to their surprise, that the Mexicans had not destroyed the bridges, but throughout the whole length of this narrow passage no person was to be seen. No one welcomed or opposed. Fiercely those stern men strode on, over the causeway and through the now deserted streets, till they entered into the encampment of their comrades.

The insurrection had been suddenly excited by an atrocious massacre on the part of Alvarado. This leader, a brave soldier, but destitute either of tact or judgment, suspected, or pretended to suspect, that the Mexican nobles were conspiring to attack him. One of their religious festivals was at hand, when all the principal nobles of the empire were to be assembled in the performance of the rites of their religion, in the court-yard of the great temple. Suddenly Alvarado came upon them, when they were thus unarmed and unsuspicious, and, cutting them off from every avenue of escape, with musketry, artillery, and the keen sabres of his horsemen, mercilessly hewed them down. Nearly six hundred of the flower of the Mexican nobility were massacred. Though Cortez was very indignant with his lieutenant when he heard this story from his lips, and exclaimed, "Your conduct has been that of a madman," he was still enraged with the Mexicans for venturiug to attack his garrison, and declared that they should feel the weight of Spanish vengeance.

In his displeasure, he refused to call upon Montezuma. Elated by the success with which he had thus far triumphed over all obstacles, and deeming the forces he now had under his command sufficient to sweep, like chaff before the whirlwind, any armies which the natives could raise, he gave free utterance to expressions of contempt for both prince and people. There had been a tacit truce between the two parties for a few days, and had Cortez disavowed the conduct of his subaltern, and pursued conciliatory measures, it is possible that the natives might again have been appeased. The insolent tone he assumed, and his loud menace of vengeance, aroused the natives anew, and they grasped their arms with a degree of determination and ferocity never manifested before.

Bernal Diaz in the following terms records this event: "Cortez asked Alvarado for what reason he fell upon the natives while they were dancing and holding a festival in honor of their gods. To this Alvarado replied that it was in order to be beforehand with them, having had intelligence of their hostile intentions toward him from two of their own nobility and a priest. Cortez then asked of him if it was true that they had requested of him permission to hold their festival. The other replied that it was so, and that it was in order to take them by surprise, and to punish and terrify them, so as to prevent their making war upon the Spaniards, that he had determined to fall on them by anticipation. At hearing this avowal, Cortez was highly enraged. He censured the conduct of Alvarado in the strongest terms, and in this temper left him.

"Some say that it was avarice which tempted Alvarado to make this attack, in order to pillage the Indians of the golden ornaments which they wore at their festival. I never heard any just reason for the assertion; nor do I believe any such thing, although it is so represented by Bartholome de las Casas. For my part, I am convinced that his intention in falling on them at that time was in order to strike terror into them, and prevent their insurrection, according to the saying that the first attack is half the battle."

CHAPTER VIII.

BATTLE OF THE DISMAL NIGHT.

THE force which Cortez now had under his command, if we take into consideration the efficiency of European discipline and of European weapons of warfare, was truly formidable. In the stone buildings which protected and encircled his encampment, he could marshal, in battle array, twelve hundred Spaniards and eight thousand native allies; but they were nearly destitute of provisions, and the natives were rapidly assembling from all quarters in countless numbers. Cortez sent four hundred men out into the streets to reconnoitre. They had hardly emerged from the walls of their fortress before they were assailed with shouts of vengeance, and a storm of arrows and javelins fell upon them. Phrenzied multitudes thronged the streets and the house-tops, and from the roofs and the summits of the temples, stones and all similar missiles were poured down upon the heads of the Spaniards. With great difficulty this strong detachment fought their way back to their fortified quarters, having lost twenty-three in killed, and a large number being wounded.

This success greatly emboldened the Mexicans, and in locust legions they pressed upon the Spanish quarters, rending the air with their unearthly shouts, and darkening the sky with their missiles. The artillery was immediately brought to bear upon them, and every volley opened immense gaps in their ranks; but the places of the dead were instantly occupied by others, and there seemed to be no end to their numbers. Never did mortal men display more bravery than these exasperated Mexicans exhibited, struggling for their homes and their rights. Twice they came very near forcing an entrance over the walls into the Spanish quarters. Had they succeeded, in a hand to hand fight numbers must have triumphed, and the Spaniards must have been inevitably destroyed; but the batteries of the Spaniards mowed down the assailants like grass before the scythe, and the Mexicans were driven from the walls. All the day long the conflict was continued, and late into the night. The ground was covered with the dead when darkness stopped the carnage.

The soldiers of Narvaez, unaccustomed to such scenes, and appalled by the fury and the number of their enemies, began to murmur loudly. They had been promised the spoils of an empire which they were assured was already conquered; instead of this, they found themselves in the utmost peril, exposed to a conflict with a vigorous and exasperated enemy, surrounding them with numbers which could not be counted. Bitterly they execrated their own folly in allowing themselves to be thus deluded; but their murmurs could now be of no avail. The only hope for the Spaniards was in united and indomitable courage.

The energies of Cortez increased with the difficulties which surrounded him. During the night he selected a strong force of picked men to make a vigorous sally in the morning. To nerve them to higher daring, he resolved to head the perilous enterprise himself. He availed himself of all his knowledge of Indian warfare, and of all the advantages which European military art could furnish. In the early dawn, these troops, in solid column, rushed from the gates of their fortress; but the foe, greatly augmented by the fresh troops which had been pouring in during the night, were ready to receive him. Both parties fought with ferocity which has never been surpassed. Cortez, to his inexpressible chagrin, found himself compelled to retire before the natives, who, in numbers perfectly amazing, were crowding upon him.

Most of the streets were traversed by canals. The bridges were broken down, and the Spaniards, thus arrested in their progress and crowded together, were overwhelmed with stones and arrows from the house-tops. Cortez set fire to the houses every where along his line of march. Though the walls of many of these buildings were of stone, the flames ran eagerly through the dry and combustible interior, and leaped from roof to roof. A wide and wasting conflagration soon swept horribly through the doomed city, adding to the misery of the bloody strife. All the day long the battle raged. The streets were strewn with the bodies of the dead, and crimsoned with gore. The natives cheerfully sacrificed a hundred of their own lives to take the life of one of their foes. The Spaniards were, however, at length driven back behind their walls, leaving twelve of their number dead in the streets, and having sixty severely wounded.

Another night darkened over the bloodstained and smouldering city. The Spaniards, exhausted by the interminable conflict, still stood fiercely behind their ramparts. The natives, in continually increasing numbers, surrounded them, filling the night air with shrieks of defiance and rage. Cortez had displayed personally the most extraordinary heroism during the protracted strife. His situation now seemed desperate. Though many thousands of the Mexicans had been slaughtered during the day, recruits flocked in so rapidly that their numbers remained undiminished. Cortez had received a severe wound in his hand which caused him intense anguish. His soldiers could hardly stand from their exhaustion. Many had been slain, and nearly all were wounded. The maddened roar of countless thousands of the fiercest warriors surging around their bulwarks almost deafened the ear. Every moment it was apprehended that the walls would be scaled, and the inundation pour in resistlessly upon them.

In this extremity Cortez decided to appeal to his captive Montezuma, and try the effect of his interposition to soothe or overawe his subjects. Assuming the tone of humanity, he affected to deplore the awful carnage which had taken place. He affirmed that the city must inevitably be destroyed entirely, and the inhabitants generally slaughtered, unless they could be induced to lay down their arms. Montezuma, from one of the towers of the Spanish fortress, had watched, with a throbbing heart and flooded eyes, the progress of the fight as the flames swept through the streets, and destruction, like a scythe, mowed down his subjects. The amiable, beloved, perplexed sovereign was thus induced, though with much hesitation, to interpose. He was adored by his people; but he believed that the Spaniards were enthroned by the voice of destiny, and that resistance would but involve the nation in a more bloody ruin.

Another morning dawned upon the combatants. In its earliest light the battle was again renewed with increasing fury. No pen can describe the tumult of this wild war. The yell of countless thousands of assailants, the clang of their trumpets, gongs, and drums, the clash of arms, the rattle of musketry, and the roar of artillery, presented a scene which had never before found a parallel in the New World.

Suddenly all the tumult was hushed as the venerated emperor, dressed in his imperial robes, appeared upon the walls, and waved his hand to command the attention of his subjects. At the sight of their beloved sovereign silence almost instantaneously prevailed, all bowed their heads in reverence, and many prostrated themselves upon the ground. Montezuma earnestly entreated them to cease from the conflict, assuring them that the Spaniards would retire from the city if the Mexicans would lay down their arms.

"The war will soon be over," a Mexican shouted from the crowd, "for we have all sworn that not a Spaniard shall leave the city alive."

As Montezuma continued his urgency, pleading for the detested Spaniards, the natives for a few moments longer continued to listen patiently. But gradually a sullen murmur, like a rising breeze, began to spread through the ranks. Reproaches and threats succeeded. Indignation now overtopped all barriers, and a shower of stones and arrows suddenly fell upon the unhappy monarch. Cortez had taken the precaution to send a body-guard upon the wall with Montezuma, with bucklers for his protection; but so sudden and unexpected was the assault, that two arrows pierced his body, and a stone, striking him on the temple, felled him

THE FALL OF MONTEZUMA.

senseless to the ground before they could raise their shields. This was the last drop in the cup of bitterness which Montezuma was doomed to drain. The wounded monarch was conveyed to his apartment, crushed in spirit, and utterly broken-hearted. Finally, resolved no longer to live, he tore the bandages from his wounds, and refused all nourishment. Silent, and brooding over his terrible calamities, he lingered, the picture of dejection and woe, for a few days, until he died.

In the mean time the battle was resumed with all its fury. Throughout the day it raged with the most intense ferocity. The Mexicans took possession of a high tower which commanded the Spanish quarters. It was necessary to dislodge them at any sacrifice. A detachment of chosen men was three times repulsed in its desperate assault. Cortez, aware that the safety of the army depended upon the result, ordered a buckler to be bound to his arm, as he could not grasp it with his wounded hand, and placed himself at the head of the attacking column. Animated by his voice and example, the Spaniards forced their way up the steps of the temple, driving the Mexicans before them. Having reached the spacious platform on the summit, a terrible strife ensued. Two young Mexican nobles resolved to effect the destruction of Cortez by the sacrifice of their own lives. They seized him, dragged him to the battlements, and threw themselves over while clinging to his person, that they might thus dash him also upon the pavement beneath. But Cortez, by his wonderful strength and agility, shook them off, and thus broke from their grasp, though they both perished. The victorious Spaniards then set fire to the tower. Other sorties were made during the day, and the wretched city was as the crater of a volcano of flame and blood. The energies of both parties seemed to redouble with despair.

At last another night spread its veil over the infuriated combatants. In its darkest watches, the indomitable Cortez made a sortie at the head of a strong band, and set three hundred buildings in flames. The lurid fire, crackling to the skies, illumined the tranquil lake, and gleamed portentously upon the most distant villages in the vast mountain-girdled valley. The tumult of the midnight assault, the shrieks of the women and children, and the groans of the wounded and the dying, blended dismally with the roar of the conflagration.

Cortez now summoned the Mexican chiefs to a parley. He stood upon the wall. The beautiful Marina, as interpreter, stood at his side. The native chiefs were upon the ground before him. The inflexible Spanish commander endeavored to intimidate his determined foes by threats.

"If you do not immediately submit," said he, "I will lay the whole city in ashes, and every man, woman, and child shall be put to the sword."

They answered defiantly,

"The bridges are broken down, and you can not escape. You have better weapons of war than we, but we have greater numbers. If we offer a thousand lives for one, we will continue the battle till you are all destroyed."

Saying this, they gave a signal, and a storm of arrows and javelins pierced the air, and fell into the beleaguered fortress. Notwithstanding the bold tone assumed by Cortez, the Spaniards were in great dismay. It was manifest to all that their destruction was certain unless they could cut their way through the enemy, and escape from the city. The extraordinary energies of this iron fanatic still remained unshaken. Calmly he reflected upon his position, examined his resources, and formed his plans. The Mexicans had barricaded the streets, and had broken down the causeways, to prevent, if possible, the escape of their foes. But there was no longer any alternative for Cortez. Destruction was certain unless he could effect his escape. He decided to make the desperate attempt at midnight. He immediately constructed moving towers, to be pushed through the streets on wheels, at the head of his columns, under the protection of which his soldiers could force their way, and make every bullet accomplish its mission. A platform on the top could be let down, affording a bridge to the roofs of the houses, thus placing the Spaniards on a level with their assailants. The sides of the towers were amply strong to repel darts and arrows. Thus protected from all harm, the sharpshooters could sweep the streets and the housetops.

At midnight the retreat was commenced in three divisions. Sandoval led the van, Alvarado the rear. Cortez took command of the centre, where he placed the distinguished prisoners, among whom were a son and daughter of Montezuma, and several of the high nobles. He also carried with his division the artillery, the baggage, and a portable bridge, ingeniously constructed of timber, to be laid over the breaches in the causeway. In profound silence the army issued from their quarters, and marched firmly along through the smouldering and gory streets.

For a little time they advanced unmolested; but the Mexicans were watching their movements, and were silently making dispositions for a tremendous onset. Suddenly the shout of an innumerable multitude and the clash of arms rose fearfully in the dark night air, and from every quarter the natives came rushing on, and stones, javelins, darts, and arrows rattled like hail-stones upon helmet and buckler. Every inch of the way was now contested. The progress of the Spaniards, though slow, was resistless, the cannon and the musketry sweeping down all obstacles.

At last they arrived at one of the numerous canals which every where intersected the city. The bridge was destroyed, and the deep waters flowing from the lake cut off all retreat. The wooden bridge, prepared for such an emergence, was thrown across the chasm. The head of the Spanish column fought its way over successfully; but, unfortunately, the weight of the artillery and of the dense throng wedged the timbers so fast into the stones that all their efforts could not again remove them. Their peril was growing every moment more imminent, as the roused natives were thronging to every point where the retiring foe could be assailed. They were thus compelled to leave the bridge behind them.

Advancing precipitately, the Spaniards soon arrived at a second breach. Here they found themselves hemmed in on all sides, and they had no means of bridging the gap; but, planting their cannon so as to hold the natives at bay, every available hand was employed in filling the chasm with stones and timbers torn from the demolished and smouldering dwellings. The labor was difficult and perilous, for they were incessantly assailed by the most pelting storm of the missiles of destruction.

For two days this terrific conflict raged. Seven breaches in the canals they were compelled thus to bridge with stones and timbers torn from the adjacent streets; but the Spaniards still slowly advanced, triumphing with difficulty over every obstacle which the natives could interpose. Though they thus sternly fought their way along, trampling beneath them the mutilated bodies of the dying and of the dead, at the close of the second day they found their foes more numerous and their situation more desperate than ever.

As the gloom of night again descended, a deeper, heavier gloom rested upon all in the heart of the Spanish camp. A wailing storm arose of wind and rain, and nature mourned and wept as if in sympathy with the woes of man. Availing themselves of the darkness and of the uproar of the midnight tempest, though weary, faint, and bleeding, they urged their steps along the war-scathed streets, for a time strangely encountering no opposition. But when they reached the long causeway, nearly two miles in length and but thirty feet wide, by which alone they could reach the land, a yell of exultation suddenly rose from the black and storm-lashed waters of the lake, loud as the heaviest thunders. The whole lake, on both sides of the causeway, seemed alive with the boats of the natives, and the Spaniards were immediately assailed by the swarming multitudes, who, in the fierce and maddened strife, set all danger at defiance.

War never exhibited a more demoniac aspect. The natives opposed their advance, crowded their rear, and clambered up the sides of the causeway, attacking the foe on each flank with indescribable fury. Fresh warriors instantly rushed into the place where their comrades had fallen, and those in the rear of the tumultuous mass crowded their companions in the front ranks resistlessly upon the compact enemy.

There were three chasms in the causeway broken by the Mexicans which the Spaniards were compelled to bridge in the darkness and the storm, and while assailed by an innumerable and almost an invisible foe. Imagination can not compass the horrors of that night. *Noche triste*, dismal night, is the name by which it has ever since been distinguished. In the awful confusion, military skill and discipline were of but little avail. The Spaniards could with difficulty distinguish friend from foe, and ere long they were nearly all quite swept away by the torrent rushing so resistlessly upon them.

Cortez succeeded in keeping about a hundred men around him, and, using the bodies of the dead to aid him in bridging two chasms, he at length reached the main land. The horrid clamor still rose from the darkness of the causeway as his companions, left behind, were struggling in desperation with the multitudes who inclosed them. Cortez heroically, with every

THE BATTLE UPON THE CAUSEWAY

man in his little band still able to fight, marched back to their rescue. A few succeeded in breaking through the enemy, and joined him. Multitudes were struck down or hurled into the lake; but dreadful was the anguish of Cortez as he heard, piercing through the clamor, the cries for help of his companions who were seized by the natives as captives, and who were being borne away to be offered in sacrifice to their gods. The few who escaped, exhausted and bleeding, clung together for the remainder of the night near the village of Tacuba, where the causeway reached the main land.

When the first gray of the lurid morning dawned, the whole length of the causeway was seen covered with the bodies of the slain. The chasms were clogged up with fragments of artillery, baggage-wagons, dead horses, and the corpses of Spaniards and natives. The features of the dead were distorted by all the hateful passions of the strife. A few only had escaped. Nearly all the horses, all the cannon, all the plundered treasure, and all the baggage-wagons, were either sunk in the lake, or were floating in fragments upon its surface. The storm had passed away, and the placid waters were blackened with the war-canoes of the natives. Not even a musket remained to the Spaniards. Bernal Diaz records that in this bloody night eight hundred and seventy of the Spaniards perished. More than four thousand of their allies were also slain.

As Cortez gazed upon the feeble band of mangled and bleeding soldiers which now alone remained to him, even his stern heart was moved, and he bowed his head and wept bitterly. We can not regret that some drops of retributive woe were wrung from the heart of that guilty conqueror. He had overwhelmed a benighted nation with misery. Under the divine government, such a crime can not go unpunished, and the penalty must descend either in this life or in that which is to come.

But this was no time to indulge in grief. It was necessary immediately to find some shelter for the wearied troops. The Mexicans were preparing to renew the attack, and the inhabitants of Tacuba were assembling in arms. At a little distance, on a rising ground, Cortez discovered a large stone temple. He immediately took possession of it, and here found not only temporary shelter, but, fortunately, provisions for his almost famished troops. Here, for a day, the Spaniards beat off the foe who incessantly assailed them.

"And God only knows," says Cortez, "the toil and fatigue with which it was accomplished; for of twenty-four horses that remained to us, there was not one that could move briskly, nor a horseman able to raise his arm, nor a foot-soldier unhurt who could make any effort."

They were now on the western side of the lake. It was necessary to pass around the northern shore of this vast expanse of water, as the country was there thinly populated, and they would be consequently less liable to attack. The road led a distance of nearly a hundred miles over mountains and through marshes to the eastern shore. From there, a march of more than sixty-four miles was necessary before they could reach the territory of Tlascala, which was the first point where they could hope for any relief.

Under the guidance of a Tlascalan soldier, the despairing band commenced its march. They advanced the first day and night but nine miles, fighting incessantly all the way. For six days, with hardly any respite, they continued their retreat. Their only food they gathered as they hurried along, of berries, roots, and green corn. They were continually assailed by the indefatigable foe; but with their few remaining horses, their steel swords, and the energies which European civilization confers, they beat off their assailants and continued their flight. As the horses were needed to beat off the swarming foe, the sick and wounded were compelled to hobble along, as they could, on crutches. "Next to God," says Cortez, "our greatest security was in our horses." One horse was killed. The Spaniards eagerly devoured his flesh, "not leaving," says Cortez, "even his skin, or any other part of him, so great were our necessities."

Cortez, who promptly recovered from his momentary weakness, manifested the utmost sereneness and imperturbability of spirit, shared every hardship of the soldiers, and maintained their confidence in him by surpassing all in the gallantry and the magnanimity of his courage.

Exhausted and wounded as they were, it required the toilsome journey of a week to reach the mountain summits which encircle the great valley of Mexico. As they approached the defiles of these mountains, parties of the enemy were seen here and there in increasing numbers. The natives shouted to them from a distance insults, defiance, and threats. Marina, who fortunately escaped the massacre of the *dismal night*, remarked that they often, in exultant tones, exclaimed,

"Hurry along, robbers, hurry along; you will soon meet with the vengeance due to your crimes."

The significance of this threat was soon made manifest. As the Spaniards were emerging from a narrow pass among the cliffs of the mountains, they came suddenly upon an extended plain. Here, to their amazement, they found an enormous army of the natives filling the whole expanse, and apparently cutting off all possibility of farther retreat. The sight was sufficient to appal the most dauntless heart. The whole plain, as far as the eye could extend, seemed as a living ocean of armed men, with its crested billows of banners, and gleaming spears, and helmets, and plumes. Even the heart of Cortez for a moment sank within him as his practiced eye told him that there were two hundred thousand warriors there in battle array, through whose serried ranks he must cut his bloody path or perish. To all the Spaniards it seemed certain that their last hour had now tolled; but each man resolved to sell his life as dearly as possible.

Cortez immediately assembled his band

around him, and invigorated them with a forcible harangue. He assured them that there was no possible hope but in the energies of despair; but that, with those energies, they might confidently expect God's blessing, for they were his servants, his missionaries, endeavoring to overthrow the idols of the heathen, and to introduce the religion of the cross. In solid column, with their long spears bristling in all directions, and clad in coats of mail which protected a great part of their bodies from both arrow and spear, they plunged desperately into the dense masses of the enemy. Wherever this solid body of iron men directed its course, the tumultuous throng of the foe was pierced and dashed aside, as the stormy billows of the ocean yield to the careering steamer. The marvelous incidents of this fight would occupy pages. The onset of the Spaniards was so fierce that the natives could present no effectual resistance; but as the Indians were compelled to retire from the front of the assailing column, they closed up with shouts of vengeance and with redoubled fury upon the flanks and the rear. Cortez had heard that the superstition of the Mexicans was such that the fate of a battle depended upon the imperial banner, which was most carefully guarded in the centre of the army. If that were taken, the natives deemed themselves forsaken by their gods, and in dismay would break and fly. In the distance, for there was no smoke of artillery to darken this field of battle, he saw this standard proudly waving in the breeze. With impetuosity which crushed down all opposition, he pushed toward it. The standard-bearers were stricken down and pinned to the earth with lances. Cortez, with his own hand, seized the sacred banner, and as he waved it aloft his soldiers raised a simultaneous shout of triumph.

The natives, with cries of rage, grief, and despair, in the wildest tumult, broke and fled to the mountains. Their gods had abandoned them. The victory of the Spaniards was complete. They record, though doubtless with exaggeration, for they had no leisure to stop and count the slain, that twenty thousand of their enemies were left dead upon that bloody field. With new alacrity the victors now pressed on, and the next day entered the territory of the Tlascalans.

Here they were received with the greatest kindness. The enmity of the Tlascalans against the Mexicans was so inveterate, and their desire to avenge the death of their countrymen so intense, that they still clung tenaciously to the Spanish alliance, with the hope that new resources might arrive which would enable the Spaniards to retrieve their fallen fortunes.

In the hospitable city of Tlascala Cortez allowed his shattered battalions that repose which was now so indispensable. Nearly all his men were suffering severely from sickness, fatigue, and wounds. But here the Spanish chieftain learned of new disasters which had befallen him. A detachment of Spanish soldiers, who were marching from Zempoalla to the capital as a re-enforcement, had been cut off by the natives and entirely destroyed. A small party, who had been sent to convey some treasures from Tlascala to Vera Cruz, had also been surprised and destroyed among the mountains. When the life of every Spaniard was of so much importance, these were, indeed, terrible additional calamities.

The companions of Cortez were now thoroughly disheartened, and were anxious to return to Vera Cruz, send a vessel to Cuba for some transports, and abandon the enterprise; but the indomitable warrior, though lying upon the bed in a raging fever, and while a surgeon was cutting off two of his mutilated and inflamed fingers, and raising a portion of the bone of his skull, which had been splintered by the club of a native, was forming his plans to return to Mexico and reconquer what he had lost. The resources at his command still appeared to him sufficient to form a nucleus around which to assemble a new army. The garrison at Vera Cruz, with its artillery and military stores, still remained unimpaired; the Tlascalans and Zempoallans continued firm in their alliance; and he still could assemble, notwithstanding his losses, as large a force as accompanied him in his first march into Mexico. He therefore resolved to make vigorous and prompt preparations to prosecute his enterprise anew. He wrote to his sovereign an account of the disasters he had encountered, saying, "I can not believe that the good and merciful God will thus suffer his cause to perish among the heathen."

With great energy and sagacity he aroused himself for this new effort. He made special exertions to secure the cordial co-operation of the Tlascalan chiefs, by distributing among them the rich spoil taken in his last battle. He dispatched four ships, selected from the fleet captured from Narvaez, to Hispaniola and Jamaica, to collect recruits and supplies. That he might secure the command of the lake, he prepared, with the ready aid of the Tlascalans, materials for building twelve vessels, to be conveyed in pieces by the men of burden to the lake, there to be put together and launched upon the waters.

The companions of Cortez had, however, by far too vivid a recollection of the horrors of the *dismal night* to participate in the zeal of their commander. Murmurs against the enterprise grew louder and louder, until the camp was almost in a state of mutiny. They assembled, and appointed a delegation to wait upon their commander, and remonstrate against another attempt, with his broken battalions, to subjugate so powerful an empire. Respectfully, but firmly, they demanded to be taken back to Cuba. All the arguments and entreaties of Cortez were of no avail to change their minds or to allay their anxieties.

We have before mentioned that a detachment of soldiers from Vera Cruz had been cut off by the natives. The assailing force was from one of the Mexican provinces in the vicinity of Tlascala, called Tepeaca. The soldiers, without much unwillingness, consented to march to their region, and chastise them for the deed. The enterprise would be attended with but little danger, and promised a large amount of booty. It was now the month of August. Cortez headed the expedition, and in the foray of a few weeks, after an enormous slaughter of the Tepeacans, reduced the province to subjection, and returned to Tlascala laden with plunder. Another foray was soon undertaken, and then another. Thus, for five months, while he was collecting recruits and accumulating supplies, he adroitly kept his men employed in various military expeditions till they again became accustomed to victory, and were ready to enter upon a wider field of glory, which should open before them more brilliant prospects for wealth. Fortune, it is said, helps those who help themselves. This inflexibility of purpose and untiring energy on the part of Cortez, was accompanied by what is usually termed the gifts of peculiarly good fortune.

The Governor of Cuba, unaware of the disaster which had befallen Narvaez, sent two ships after him with a supply of men and military stores. These vessels were decoyed into the harbor of Vera Cruz, the stores seized, and the men were easily induced to enter into the service of Cortez.

The Governor of Jamaica fitted out an expedition of three ships to prosecute an expedition of discovery and conquest. They were very unfortunate, and, after many disasters, these ships, their crews being almost in a famishing state, cast anchor at Vera Cruz. They listened eagerly to the brilliant prospects which Cortez held out to them, and enlisted under his banner. At the same time, it also happened that a ship arrived from Spain, fitted out by some private merchants with military stores, and other articles for traffic among the natives. Cortez immediately purchased the cargo, and induced the crew to follow the example of the others, and join his army. At last, the agents he sent to Hispaniola and Jamaica returned, with two hundred soldiers, eighty horses, two battering-cannon, and a considerable supply of ammunition and muskets. Cortez had in these various ways now collected about him eight hundred and eighteen foot-soldiers, eighty-six horsemen, three battering-cannon, and fifteen field-pieces.

He established his head-quarters at Tepeaca, on a small river which ran into the lake. The iron, the planks, the timber, the masts, the cordage, and the materials necessary to construct and equip a fleet of thirteen brigantines, were to be carried a distance of sixty miles, over rough roads, on the shoulders of men. Eight thousand *men of burden* were furnished by the Tlascalans for this work. Tepeaca was two miles from the shore of the lake, and the rivulet upon which it was situated was shallow. A large number of natives were employed for two months in deepening the channel, that the vessels might be floated down. Though the Mexicans made many attacks while the brigantines were being built, they were invariably repulsed. At length the fleet was finished, and the whole army was drawn up to witness, with all the accompaniments of religious and military pomp, the launching of the ships. Each vessel received a baptismal name and a blessing from Father Olmedo. They glided smoothly down the river, and were wafted out upon the lake, a fleet amply strong to set all the power of the Mexicans at defiance. A general shout of joy burst from the lips of the Spaniards and Tlascalans as they observed the triumphant success of this measure. All despondency now disappeared, and, sanguine of success, the whole army was eager again to march to the assault of the capital.

CHAPTER IX.

THE CAPITAL BESIEGED AND CAPTURED.

WHILE Cortez was thus vigorously preparing to renew the assault upon the city of Mexico, the Mexicans were no less busy in their preparations for defense. Upon the death of Montezuma, the crown passed to his more warlike brother Cuitlahua. By his energies the Spaniards had been driven from the metropolis, and he immediately, with great vigor, fortified the city anew, and recruited and drilled his armies, now familiar with the weapons of European warfare. He sent an embassy to the Tlascalans, urging alliance against a common foe, and endeavoring to incite them to rise and crush the Spaniards, who, without their alliance, would have been entirely helpless. The sagacity of Cortez, however, baffled these efforts, and he succeeded in binding the Tlascalans to him by still stronger ties.

Among other woes, the Spaniards had introduced the small-pox into Mexico. The terrible curse now swept like a blast of destruction through the land. The natives perished by thousands. Many cities and villages were almost depopulated. The fearful pestilence reached the Mexican capital, and the emperor, Cuitlahua, soon fell a victim to its ravages.

Guatemozin, the son-in-law of Montezuma, was then, by the unanimous acclaim of his countrymen, placed upon the throne. He was a young man of high reputation for ability and force of character, and proved himself the worthy leader of his nation in this dreadful crisis of its fate. Guatemozin assembled all his forces in the capital, as the strongest point upon which they could stand upon their defense.

Cortez decided to make the assault by three divisions of the army, each marching over one of the causeways. Sandoval was to command on the north, Alvarado on the west, and Olid on the south. Cortez reserved to himself the command of the brigantines, which were to sweep the lakes, and drive the war-canoes of the natives from the causeways. Each brigantine was manned with twenty-five Spaniards, and armed with a cannon, whose shot would make fearful havoc among the frail and crowded canoes of the Mexicans.

Guatemozin immediately foresaw how much he had to dread from this fleet, and decided that, at every hazard, he must attempt its destruction. He accordingly assembled an enormous mass of canoes, hoping by numbers to overpower the enemy. The day was calm; not a ripple disturbed the glassy surface of the water, when a fleet of canoes, in numbers which could not be counted, pushed out boldly into the lake to assail the brigantines lying at anchor.

But just then, to the great joy of the Spaniards and to the dismay of the Mexicans, a fresh and favorable breeze arose, which would drive the brigantines resistlessly through the swarm of fragile boats which were approaching them. The sails were instantly spread, the cannon were loaded almost to the muzzle, and the work of death began. The heavy vessels crushed the canoes, overturned them, drove them one upon another in indescribable confusion, while the merciless shot pierced bones, and nerves, and sinews, and the surface of the lake was covered with the mutilated bodies of the dying and of the dead. The water was red with blood, and in a short time the fleet was destroyed; but few of the boats escaped. The

Mexicans, from their house-tops, gazed with dismay upon this awful scene of carnage, and were oppressed with fearful forebodings that no degree of courage and no superiority of numbers could avail them against the terrible engines of destruction which European skill had framed.

Cortez was now completely master of the lake. He formed his brigantines into three divisions, to cover the assailants on the three causeways and to protect them from any attack by canoes. He thus also preserved communication, prompt and effective, between the different divisions of his army. The military skill displayed by Cortez in all these arrangements is of the highest kind. The conquest of Mexico was not achieved by accident, but by sagacity, persevering energy, and patient toil almost unparalleled.

The siege was now prosecuted with the most determined vigor. The approaches were made along the three causeways. The natives had broken down the bridges and reared a succession of formidable barricades, and as they were driven from one by the irresistible force of artillery, they retired, with firmness worthy of admiration, to the next, there to maintain their post to the last possible moment. The brigantines approached the sides of the causeways and opened a destructive fire upon the valiant defenders, where the Spaniards were exposed to no danger in return. Thus for nearly three months, by day and by night, on the land and on the water, the bloody strife was continued.

Cortez was astonished at the obstinacy and efficiency of the resistance effected by the besieged. Gradually, however, the besiegers advanced, carefully filling up behind them the gaps in the causeway, that they might easily, if necessary, effect a retreat. They were taught the necessity of this precaution by a terrible repulse which they at one time encountered. Guatemozin, with a quick military eye, perceiving that the causeway occupied by one of the divisions of the Spaniards was impassable behind the Spaniards from trenches unfilled, and broken bridges, and the ruins of barricades, ordered the Mexican troops to retire, to lure the Spaniards forward. He then collected an enormous force, dispatching some in canoes along shallows which the brigantines could not approach, and then, at a signal from the great alarm drum on the summit of the temple, whose doleful tones could be heard for miles, the whole mass, with frantic rage, stimulated by hope, rushed upon the foe. The sudden assault, so impetuous, and sustained by such vast numbers, was quite successful. The Spaniards were driven back in confusion, horsemen and infantry crowding upon each other, till multitudes were forced, pell-mell, horses, and cannon, and men, into the chasms. Here the natives, in their light canoes, fell furiously upon them. More than twenty Spaniards were killed outright, and forty, mangled and bleeding, fell alive into the hands of the victors. There was no possible escape for the captives from their doom. They were to be sacrificed to the gods.

This was an awful reverse, and the Spaniards were horror-stricken in contemplating the fate of their captured comrades. The capital was that night illuminated with great brilliance, and the splendor of the great pyramidal temple, blazing with innumerable torches, gleamed far and wide over the lake. It was an awful spectacle to the Spaniards, for they well knew the scenes which were transpiring on that lofty altar of idolatry. The preparations for the sacrifice could be distinctly seen, and the movements of the sacrificial priests. The white bodies of the victims could also be clearly discerned as they were stripped naked for the torture and the knife; and when the awful torture was applied, the shrieks of the wretched sufferers pierced the still night air, and penetrated the camp of the Spaniards. They listened appalled to those cries of agony, imagining that they could distinguish each victim by the sound of his voice.

This awful scene is thus described by Diaz: "On a sudden, our ears were struck by the horrific sound of the great drum, the timbrels, horns, and trumpets on the temple. We all directed our eyes thither, and, shocking to relate, saw our unfortunate countrymen driven by blows to the place where they were to be sacrificed, which bloody ceremony was accompanied by the dismal sound of all the instruments of the temple. We perceived that when they had brought the wretched victims to the flat summit of the body of the temple, they put plumes upon their heads, and made them dance before their accursed idols. When they had done this, they laid them upon their backs on the stone used for the purpose, where they cut out their hearts alive, and having presented them, yet palpitating, to their gods, they drew the bodies down the steps by the feet, where they were taken by others of their priests. Let the reader think what were our sensations on this occasion. O heavenly God! said we to ourselves, do not suffer us to be sacrificed by these wretches. Do not suffer us to die so cruel a death. And then, how shocking a reflection, that we were unable to relieve our poor friends, who were thus murdered before our eyes."

This victory elated the Mexicans exceedingly. They cut off the heads of the sacrificed Spaniards, and sent them to the adjacent provinces, to prove that their gods, now appeased by this signal offering of blood, had abandoned the enemy. The priests sent the assurance far and wide that victory was now certain, as the oracles had returned the response that in eight days the detested enemy should be entirely destroyed. This prediction exerted a great influence upon a superstitious people. Many of the natives who had joined Cortez deserted his cause, and even the Tlascalans began to waver. The prudence and shrewdness of Cortez again met the danger and averted it. For eight days he made no advance, but merely stood on the defensive. The predicted time having expired, he said, "You see that the gods have deceived the Mexicans. They have espoused our cause."

The fickle people immediately returned to their stations, and others joined them, so that Cortez, according to his own account, now found himself at the head of one hundred and fifty thousand Indians. Gomara and Herrera assert that there were not less than two hundred thousand. The number of defenders in the Mexican capital can not with accuracy be ascertained. It is estimated, however, from various considerations, that there must have been at least two hundred thousand.

The Spaniards, in this sanguinary and protracted siege, often suffered severely for want of food. With apparent reluctance, the historians of the expedition record that their Indian auxiliaries found quite an abundant supply for themselves in the bodies of their enemies. Some of them were rather ashamed to acknowledge that their auxiliaries were inveterate cannibals. Cortez, however, alludes to their horrible repasts quite in a tone of indifference.

With greater caution the Spaniards now advanced, fortifying every point they gained, and preparing a smooth and unobstructed road in their rear. Their progress was exceedingly slow, and it was necessary to adopt every possible precaution against an enemy who had manifested such unexpected audacity and skill. As the Spaniards pushed forward, the Mexicans, contesting every inch of the way, sullenly retired, rearing barricade after barricade, and digging ditch behind ditch. But artillery and European science were sure, in the end, to triumph. Gradually the three divisions of the army forced their way across the causeways, and entered the streets of the city. But here the defense was, if possible, still more determined and sanguinary. Every street was a guarded defile, where every obstacle was interposed which Mexican military skill could devise. Every house was a fortress, from whose battlemented roof and loop-holed windows a shower of stones, arrows, and javelins fell upon the besiegers. As the Spaniards gained ground, step by step, they leveled every house, and left entire ruin and desolation behind them.

Day after day and week after week of this unparalleled siege lingered along, every hour of which almost was a battle. The Mexicans fell in incredible numbers. The horrors of pestilence and famine in the pent-up city were soon added to the awful carnage and misery of war.

The brigantines swept the lake, cutting off nearly all supplies by water for the valiant yet starving defenders, while the armies on the causeways completely invested the city by land. Wan and haggard, these unhappy victims of European aggression, even when all hope of successful resistance had expired, heroically resolved to perish to the last man, and to bury themselves beneath the ruins of their city.

Even the heart of Cortez was touched with the almost unearthly misery he was inflicting upon an unoffending people. Again and again he sent to Guatemozin demanding capitulation; but the proud Mexican monarch rejected every overture with indignation and scorn. At length the three divisions of the army, from their three different points of attack, penetrated the city so far as to meet at the great public square. The whole western portion of the city was now in the power of the besiegers. The starving and dying defenders were shut up in a small section of less than one fourth of the capital.

The Spaniards, now sure of success, pressed the siege with new ardor. Their forces had met, and were combined in the great square. The avenues connecting with the country were all open before them, so that they could freely go and come. The lake was swept by the brigantines, and, though a swift canoe could occasionally shoot along the shore, the natives could not venture, in the face of such a force, to cross the wide expanse of water. Affairs in the Mexican camp were now in the very darkest state of misery and gloom.

The Mexicans regarded their monarch with superstitious veneration. Upon his life all their destinies were suspended. His voice was omnipotent with the people. After long deliberation, the desperate resolve was adopted to send Guatemozin in a canoe across the broad waters of the lake, which like an ocean swept around the city, to the eastern shore. But Cortez, ever on the alert, anticipated this movement, and ordered the brigantines to maintain the most vigilant watch. The Mexicans, to deceive Cortez, sent an embassy to him to confer upon terms of capitulation. They hoped thus to engage his attention so that Guatemozin could escape unperceived, and, having roused all the distant provinces, who would spring to arms at his voice, could make an assault upon the rear of the foe.

Sandoval was now placed in command of the brigantines. He observed one morning several canoes, crowded with people and plied by strong rowers, shoot from the city, and direct their course across the lake toward the eastern shore. The signal was instantly given for pursuit. Unfortunately for the Mexicans, a favorable breeze sprang up, and one of the brigantines soon drew near the largest boat. The cannon was loaded, and heavily shotted and aimed. The gunner stood ready with his lighted torch. In another moment the fatal discharge would have strewed the lake with the fragments of the boat and the mangled bodies of the slain. The Mexicans, regardless of their own lives, but intensely anxious for the safety of their sovereign, dropped their oars, and holding up their hands beseechingly, with cries and tears, besought the Spaniards not to fire, exclaiming that the emperor was there.

Eagerly the precious prize was seized. The heroic Guatemozin with dignity surrendered himself into the hands of his victors, asking no favor for himself, but simply requesting that no insult might be offered to the empress or his children, who were in the boat with him. With much exultation, the captive monarch, who was but twenty-four years of age, was conveyed to the shore, and conducted into the presence of

THE CAPTURE OF GUATEMOZIN.

Cortez. Guatemozin retained his fortitude unshaken. Looking firmly upon his conqueror, he said, loftily,

"I have done what became a monarch. I have defended my people to the last extremity. Nothing now remains for me but to die. Take this dagger," he continued, placing his hand upon the one which Cortez wore at his side, "and plunge it into my bosom, and thus end a life which is henceforth useless."

Cortez well knew how to act the part of magnanimity. He was by instinct a man of princely manners. Castilian grace and dignity ever shone pre-eminent in his movements. He endeavored to console his vanquished foe, whose bold defense commanded his respect.

"You are not my captive," said he, "but the prisoner of the greatest monarch of Europe. From his great clemency, you may hope not only that you may be restored to liberty, but that you may again be placed upon the throne which you have so valiantly defended."

Guatemozin had no confidence in the word of Cortez. He knew well the perfidy and the treachery which had marked every step of the invader's march thus far. Proudly disdaining to manifest any concern for his own fate, he plead only that Cortez would be merciful to his suffering people. The conqueror promised compassion if Guatemozin would command their instant surrender. This was promptly done, and the command was instantly obeyed. The Mexicans lost all heart as soon as they learned that their monarch was a prisoner. Cortez immediately took possession of the small portion of the city which still remained undestroyed.

Thus terminated this memorable siege, one of the most remarkable which has been recorded in the horrid annals of war. It had continued for seventy-five days of almost incessant conflict. Almost every hour the fiercest battle raged, as step by step the assailants, with the utmost effort and difficulty, crowded back the valiant defenders. No less than one hundred and fifty thousand Mexicans perished in this awful and atrocious siege. The Spaniards, who wished to make their loss appear as small as possible, admit that one hundred of the Spanish soldiers fell, and many thousands of their allies.

Nearly the whole capital was now but a mass of blackened and smouldering ruins. Its numerous squares, streets, and courts, but recently so beautiful in their neat order, and their embellishments of shrubbery and flowers, were now clotted with blood and covered with the mangled bodies of the slain. The sight was hideous even to those accustomed to all the revolting scenes which demoniac war ever brings in its train.

The ground was covered with the dead. Among the putrefying heaps some wretches were seen, wounded, bleeding, and crawling about in advanced stages of those loathsome diseases produced by famine and misery.

The air was so polluted with the masses of the dead, decaying beneath the rays of a tropical sun, that Cortez was compelled to withdraw his army from the city that the dead might be removed and the streets purified. For three days and three nights the causeways were thronged by endless processions of the natives bearing the mouldering corpses from the city. But the Spaniards were insensible to the woes which they had inflicted upon others in their exultation over their great victory. They had conquered the enemy. The capital was in their hands, and they had now but to collect the boundless treasures which they supposed were accumulated in the halls of Montezuma. It was on Tuesday, the 13th of August, 1521, that the conflict ceased. The mighty empire of Mexico on that day perished, and there remained in its stead but a colony of Spain.

On the very day of the capture Cortez searched every spot where treasure could be found, and having collected every thing of value, returned to his camp, "giving thanks," he says, "to our Lord for so signal a reward and so desirable a victory as he has granted us." He continued for three or four days searching eagerly for spoils, amid all the scenes of horror presented by the devastated city. All the gold and silver which were found were melted down, and one fifth was set apart for the King of Spain, while the rest was divided among the Spaniards according to their rank and services.

"Among the spoils obtained in the city," says Cortez, in his dispatch to Charles V., "were many shields of gold, plumes, panaches, and other articles of so wonderful a character, that language will not convey an idea of them, nor could a correct conception be formed of their rare excellence without seeing them."

Still the booty which was gained fell far short of the expectation of the victors. The heroic Guatemozin, when the hope of successful defense had expired, determined that the conquerors should not be enriched by the treasures of the empire. A vast amount was consequently sent out in boats, and sunk to the bottom of the lake. For a short time, however, exultation in view of their great victory caused both the commander and his soldiers to forget their disappointment; love of glory for a moment triumphed over avarice.

The native allies had been but tools in the hand of Cortez to subjugate the Mexicans. The deluded natives had thus also subjugated themselves. They were now powerless, and the bond-servants of the Spaniards. Cortez allowed them to sack the few remaining dwellings of the smouldering capital, and to load themselves with such articles as might seem valuable to semi-barbarian eyes, but which would have no cash value in Spain. With this share of the plunder they were satisfied, and their camp resounded with revelry as those fierce warriors, with songs and dances, exulted over the downfall of their ancient foes. Cortez thanked them for their assistance, praised them for their valor, and told them that they might now go home. They went home, soon to find that it was to them home no more. The stranger possessed their country, and they and their children were his slaves.

In the Spanish camp the victory was honored by a double celebration. The first was purely worldly, and religion was held entirely in abeyance. Bonfires blazed. Deep into the night the drunken revelry resounded over the lake, until Father Olmedo remonstrated against such godless wassail.

The next day was appropriated to the religious celebration. The whole army was formed into a procession. The image of the peaceful Virgin was decorated with tattered, blackened, and bloodstained banners, beneath which the Christians had so successfully struggled against the heathen. With hymns and chants, and in the repetition of creeds and prayers, this piratic band of fanatics, crimson with the blood of the innocent, moved to an appointed sanctuary, where Father Olmedo preached an impressive sermon, and solemnized the ordinance of the mass. The sacrament was administered to Cortez and his captains, and, with the imposing accompaniments of martial music and pealing artillery, thanksgivings were offered to God.

Bernal Diaz gives the following quaint and graphic account of these festivities: "After having returned thanks to God, Cortez determined to celebrate his success by a festival in Cuyoacan. A vessel had arrived at Villa Rica with a cargo of wine, and hogs had been provided from the island of Cuba. To this entertainment he invited all the officers of his army, and also the soldiers of estimation. All things being prepared, on the day appointed we waited on our general.

"When we came to sit down to dinner, there were not tables for one half of us. This brought on great confusion among the company, and, indeed, for many reasons, it would have been much better let alone. The *plant of Noah* was the cause of many fooleries and worse things. It made some leap over the tables who afterward could not go out at the doors, and many rolled down the steps. The private soldiers swore they would buy horses with golden harness. The cross-bow-men would use none but golden arrows. All were to have their fortunes made.

"When the tables were taken away, the soldiers danced in their armor with the ladies, as many of them as there were, but the disproportion in numbers was very great. This scene was truly ridiculous. I will not mention the names; suffice it to say, a fair field was open for satire. Father Olmedo thought what he observed at the feast and in the dances too scandalous, and complained to Sandoval. The latter directly told Cortez how the reverend father was scolding and grumbling.

"Cortez, discreet in all his actions, immediately went to Father Olmedo, and, affecting to disapprove of the whole affair, requested that he would order a solemn mass and thanksgiving, and preach a sermon to the soldiers of the moral and religious duties. Father Olmedo was highly pleased at this, thinking it had originated spontaneously from Cortez, and not knowing that the hint had been given him by Sandoval. Accordingly, the crucifixes and the image of Our Lady were borne in solemn procession, with drums and standards. The Litany was sung during the ceremony. Father Olmedo preached and administered the sacrament, and we returned thanks to God for our victory."

But now came the hour for discontent and murmuring. The excitement was over, the din of arms was hushed, the beautiful city was entirely destroyed, and two hundred thousand of the wretched inhabitants, whose only crime against the Spaniards was that they defended their wives, their children, and their homes, were festering in the grave. In counting up their gains, these guilty men found that the whole sum amounted to but about one hundred and twenty thousand dollars. Their grievous disappointment vented itself in loud complainings, and was soon turned into rage. They accused Guatemozin of having secreted the treasure which had been hoarded up, and demanded that he should be put to the torture to compel him to disclose the place of concealment. Cortez, for a time, firmly refused to yield to this atrocious demand; but the clamor of the disaffected grew louder and louder, until at last Cortez was accused of being in agreement with Guatemozin, that he might appropriate to his own use the secreted treasure.

Thus goaded, Cortez infamously consented that the unhappy captive monarch should be put to the torture. The cacique of Tacuba, the companion of Guatemozin, and his highest officer, was put to the torture with him. A hot fire was kindled, and the feet of the wretched victims, drenched in oil, were exposed to the burning coals. Guatemozin had nothing to reveal. He could merely assert that the treasures of the city were thrown into the lake.

With extraordinary fortitude he endured the agony, adding additional lustre to a name already ennobled by the heroism with which he conducted the defense. His companion died upon this bed of agony. In the extremity of his torment, he turned an imploring eye toward the king. Guatemozin, it is recorded, observing his look, replied, "Am I, then, reposing upon a bed of flowers?" Cortez, who had reluctantly yielded to this atrocity, at last interposed, and rescued the imperial sufferer. Cortez has much to answer for before the bar of this world's judgment. For many of his criminal acts some apology may be framed, but for the torture of Guatemozin he stands condemned without excuse. No voice will plead his cause. Cortez seemed to be fully aware that it was not a creditable story for him to tell, and in his dispatches to the King of Spain he made no allusion to the event.

It was a grievous disappointment to Cortez that so little treasure was obtained, for his ambition was roused to send immense sums to the Spanish court, that he might purchase high favor with his monarch by thus proving the wealth and grandeur of the kingdom he had subjugated. Cortez himself accompanied a party of practiced divers upon the lake, and long and anxiously conducted the search; but the divers invariably returned from the oozy bottom of the lake empty-handed: no treasure could be found.

It has before been mentioned that the empire of Mexico consisted of a conglomeration of once independent nations, which had been in various ways annexed to the mammoth empire. It was somewhat like Austria, having many Hungarys and Polands ripe for revolt. Cortez had adroitly availed himself of these disaffections in accomplishing his wonderful conquest. The Zempoallans and Tlascalans augmented his ranks with fierce warriors nearly two hundred thousand in number. There were many provinces of the empire on the north and the west which as yet no European foot had ever entered. It was a question whether these remote provinces would band together in hostility to the Spaniards, and thus indefinitely protract the conflict, or whether, seeing the capital in ruins and their monarch a captive, they would admit the hopelessness of the strife, and yield to their conquerors.

Far and wide, through the valleys and over the mountains, the tidings of the annihilation of the Mexican army was borne by the Indian runners, awakening consternation every where in view of the resistless power of the victors. Some, however, who were restive under the Mexican yoke, were not unwilling to exchange masters. To the great relief and joy of Cortez, day after day, envoys flocked to his presence from powerful nations to proffer allegiance and implore clemency. Cortez received them all with great courtesy and hospitality, and took not a little pleasure in witnessing the amazement with which these embassadors contemplated the power, to them supernatural, which the Spaniards wielded. The brigantines spread their sails and plowed their way, with speed which no canoe could equal, over the foamy waters of the lake. The cavalry wheeled and charged in all those prompt and orderly evolutions to which the war-horse can be trained. And when the heavy artillery uttered its roar, and shivered the distant rock with its thunderbolt, the envoys, amazed, bewildered, and appalled, were prepared to make any concessions rather than incur the displeasure of such fearful foes.

The power of Cortez was now unquestioned, and Mexico was in the dust before him. Still, the conqueror was in great perplexity respecting the light in which his conduct was viewed in the court of his stern monarch, Charles V. While engaged in the slaughter of two or three hundred thousand people, while overrunning nations and establishing new governments, he was acting not only without authority from his government, but in direct opposition to its commands. Velasquez, the governor of Cuba, was invested with authority by the voice of the emperor, and yet Cortez had set his power at defiance. By the command of the emperor, expeditions had been fitted out to prosecute discoveries and to acquire dominion in Mexico, and yet Cortez had audaciously made war upon these bands marching under the banner of Spain. He had slain many, taken the rest prisoners, and constrained them, by bribes and menaces, to join his marauding army. Cortez well knew that this was treason, and that he was liable to answer for it with his life. He well knew that Velasquez, mortified and exasperated, had made bitter complaints against him at court, and that there was no one there effectually to plead his cause.

Under these circumstances, Cortez awaited with much solicitude the next arrival from

Spain. In the mean time, he made every possible effort to transmit gold and silver to the Spanish monarch, and with untiring zeal urged his discoveries, that he might ennoble himself and win the gratitude of his sovereign by adding to the wealth, the dominion, and the fame of his native kingdom. Wishing to assume that he was acting humbly as the servant of his king, he sent him, in the form of dispatches, a minute account of all his movements.

As a specimen of these dispatches, the reader will peruse with interest the following account of the last two days of the siege. This dispatch is dated from the *City of Cuyoacan* (*Mexico*), *May* 15*th*, 1522. This city was on the main land, at the end of one of the causeways which led to the island capital. The letter is thus humbly addressed:

"Most high and potent Prince; most catholic and invincible Emperor, King, and Lord."

This narrative of the siege is so minute as to occupy one hundred and fifty closely-printed octavo pages, and gives a circumstantial account of the proceedings of each day. The closing paragraphs only are here extracted. The narrative which Cortez gives sometimes differs, in unimportant particulars, from that recorded by other historians of the campaign, who were eye-witnesses of the scenes which they described.

"As soon as it was day, I caused our whole force to be in readiness, and the heavy guns to be brought out. The day before, I had ordered Pedro de Alvarado to wait for me in the square of the market-place, and not to attack the enemy until I arrived. Being all assembled, and the brigantines drawn up ready for action on the right of the houses situated on the water, where the enemy were stationed, I directed that when they heard the discharge of a musket, the land force should enter the small part of the city that remained to be taken, and drive the enemy toward the water, where the brigantines lay. I enjoined much upon them to look for Guatemozin, and endeavor to take him alive, as in that case the war would cease. I then ascended a terrace, and, before the combat began, addressed some of the nobles whom I knew, asking them for what reason their sovereign refused to come to me when they were reduced to such extremities, adding that there was no good cause why they should all perish, and that they should go and call him, and have no fears.

"Two of the principal nobles then went to

call the emperor. After a short time they returned, accompanied by one of the most considerable of their personages, Ciquacoacin, a captain and governor over them all, by whose counsels the whole affairs of the war were conducted. I received him with great kindness, that he might feel perfectly secure and free from apprehensions. At last he said that 'the emperor would by no means come into my presence, preferring rather to die; that his determination grieved him much, but that I must do whatever I desired.' When I saw that this was his settled purpose, I told the noble messenger to return to his friends, and prepare for the renewal of the war, which I was resolved to continue until their destruction was complete. So he departed.

"More than five hours had been spent in these conferences, during which time many of the inhabitants were crowded together upon piles of the dead; some were on the water, and others were seen swimming about or drowning in the part of the lake where the canoes were lying, which was of considerable extent. Indeed, so excessive were the sufferings of the people, that no one could imagine how they were able to sustain them; and an immense multitude of men, women, and children were compelled to seek refuge with us, many of whom, in their eagerness to reach us, threw themselves into the water, and were drowned among the mass of dead bodies. It appeared that the number of persons who had perished, either from drinking salt water, from famine or pestilence, amounted altogether to more than fifty thousand souls.

"In order to conceal their necessitous condition from our knowledge, the bodies of the dead were not thrown into the water, lest the brigantines should come in contact with them, nor were they taken away from the places where they had died, lest we should see them about the city; but in those streets where they had perished we found heaps of dead bodies so frequent, that a person passing could not avoid stepping upon them; and when the people of the city flocked toward us, I caused Spaniards to be stationed through all the streets to prevent our allies from destroying the wretched persons who came out in such multitudes. I also charged the captains of our allies to forbid, by all means in their power, the slaughter of these fugitives; yet all my precautions were insufficient to prevent it, and that day more than fifteen thousand lost their lives. At the same time, the better classes and the warriors of the city were pent up within narrow limits, confined to a few terraces and houses, or sought refuge on the water; but no concealment prevented our seeing their miserable condition and weakness with sufficient clearness.

"As the evening approached and no sign of their surrender appeared, I ordered the two pieces of ordnance to be leveled toward the enemy, to try their effect in causing them to yield; but they suffered greater injury when full license was given to the allies to attack them than from the cannon, although the latter did them some mischief. As this was of little avail, I ordered the musketry to be fired. When a certain angular space, where they were crowded together, was gained, and some of the people thrown into the water, those that remained there yielded themselves prisoners without a struggle.

"In the mean time, the brigantines suddenly entered that part of the lake, and broke through the midst of the fleet of canoes, the warriors who were in them not daring to make any resistance. It pleased God that the captain of a brigantine, named Garci Holguin, came up to hind a canoe in which there seemed to be persons of distinction ; and when the archers, who were stationed in the bow of the brigantine, took aim at those in the canoe, they made a signal that the emperor was there, that the men might not discharge their arrows. Instantly our people leaped into the canoe, and seized in it Guatemozin and the Lord of Tacuba, together with other distinguished persons who accompanied the emperor.

"Immediately after this occurrence, Garci Holguin, the captain, delivered to me, on a terrace adjoining the lake, where I was standing, Guatemozin, with other noble prisoners. As I, without showing any asperity of manner, bade him sit down, he came up to me and said, in his own tongue,

"'That he had done all that was incumbent on him in defense of himself and his people, until he was reduced to his present condition; that now I might do with him as I pleased.' He then laid his hand on a poniard that I wore, telling me to strike him to the heart.

"I spoke encouragingly to him, and bade him have no fears. Thus, the emperor being taken a prisoner, the war ceased at this point, which it pleased God our Lord to bring to a conclusion on Tuesday, St. Hippolytus's day, the thirteenth of August, 1521; so that from the day in which the city was first invested, the 3d of May in that year, until it was taken, seventy-five days had elapsed, during which time your majesty will see what labors, dangers, and calamities your subjects endured, and their deeds afford the best evidence how much they exposed their lives."

For three hundred years, while Mexico remained under Spanish rule, the anniversary of this victory was regularly celebrated with all the accompaniments of national rejoicing.

CHAPTER X.

THE CONQUEST CONSUMMATED.

WITH zeal and energy which never slept, Cortez fitted out several expeditions to explore the country, to study its geography, and to ascertain its resources. One party, ascending the heights of the Cordilleras, gazed with delight upon the placid expanse of the Pacific Ocean, and, descending the western declivity, planted the cross upon the sandy shores of that hitherto unknown sea. Cortez was exceedingly elated with this discovery, for he considered it another bribe with which to purchase the favor of his sovereign. He immediately made arrangements for establishing a colony on the Pacific shores, and ordered four vessels to be built to prosecute farther discoveries. He lost no time in transmitting to the emperor the tidings of this great achievement.

"I have received, most powerful sire," he wrote, "some account of another sea to the south, and learned that at two or three points it was twelve, thirteen, and fourteen days' journey from this city. The information gave me much pleasure, for it appeared to me that the discovery would prove a great and signal service to your majesty, especially as all who possess any knowledge or experience in navigation to the Indies have considered it certain that the discovery of the South Sea in these parts would bring to light many islands rich in gold, pearls, precious stones, and spiceries, together with many other unknown and choice productions. The same has been affirmed also by persons versed in learning and skilled in the science of cosmography. With such views, and a desire that I might render your majesty a distinguished and memorable service in this matter, I dispatched four Spaniards, two by one route and two by another, who, having obtained the necessary information as to the course they were to take, set out, accompanied by several of our allies as guides and companions. I ordered them not to stop until they had reached the sea, and when they had discovered it, to take actual and corporal possession in the name of your majesty.

"One of these parties traveled about one hundred and thirty leagues, through many fine provinces, without encountering any obstacles, and arrived at the sea, of which they took possession, and, in token thereof, set up crosses along the coast. After some days they returned with an account of their discovery, and informed me very particularly concerning it. They brought with them several of the natives from that quarter, together with good specimens of gold from the mines found in the provinces through which they passed, which, with other specimens, I now send to your majesty.

"The other party were absent somewhat longer, for they took a different course, and traveled one hundred and fifty leagues before they reached the sea, of which they also took possession, and brought me a full account of the coast, with some of the natives of the country. I received the strangers in both parties graciously, and having informed them of the great power of your majesty, and made them some presents, I suffered them to depart on their return to their own country, and they went away much gratified.

"In my former relation, most catholic sire, I informed your majesty that, at the time when the Indians defeated me, and first drove us out of the city of Tenochtitlan, all the provinces subject to that city rebelled against your majesty and made war upon us; and your majesty will see, by this relation, how we have reduced to your royal service most of the provinces that proved rebellious.

"As the city," he continues, "of Tenochtitlan was a place of great celebrity and distinction, and ever memorable, it appeared to me that it would be well to build another town upon its ruins. I therefore distributed the ground among the proposed inhabitants, and appointed alcaldes and regidores in the name of your majesty, according to the custom of your realms; and while the houses were going up, we determined to abide in the city of Cuyoacan, where we at present are. It is now four or five months since the rebuilding of the city was commenced, and it is already very handsome. Your majesty may be assured that it will go on increasing to such a degree that, as it was formerly the capital and mistress of all these provinces, it will still be so hereafter. It is built so far and will be completed in such a manner as to render the Spaniards strong and secure, greatly superior to the natives, and wholly unassailable by them."

The power of Cortez was now unlimited. The whole native population were virtually his slaves. He had the address to secure the friendly co-operation of the principal chiefs, and the Indians, in any numbers which he required, were driven by them to their reluctant toil. The Spaniards assumed the office of overseers, while the natives performed all the menial and painful labor. Timber was cut and dragged by the *men of burden* from the adjacent forests, and from the ruins of Tenochtitlan the new and beautiful city of Mexico rose as by magic.

Charles V., King of Spain and Emperor of Germany, was overwhelmed by the cares of his enormous empire. The scenes transpiring far away in the wilderness of the New World, important as they were, could claim but a small share of his attention. Velasquez succeeded in gaining very influential friends at court, and plied all his energies, with untiring diligence, to secure the disgrace of Cortez. Pride, ambition, and revenge alike inspired him to work, if possible, the ruin of the bold adventurer who had set his power at defiance. The sovereign was at this time in Germany, and the reins of government in Spain were temporarily placed in the hands of Adrian, who had been private tutor of the emperor.

Influenced by the coadjutors of Velasquez,

Adrian issued a warrant, signed at Burgos on the 11th of April, 1521, which, after recapitulating the offenses of which Cortez had been guilty against the majesty of the Spanish government, appointed a commissioner to repair to Mexico, seize the person of Cortez, suspend him from his functions, sequestrate his property, and bring him to trial upon the weighty charges contained in the indictment.

The accomplishment of a task so difficult required a man of consummate tact and energy; but, unfortunately, the agent selected was totally unqualified for his task. Christoval de Tapia, the appointed commissioner, was a feeble, fussy old man, a government inspector of metals in Saint Domingo. He landed at Vera Cruz in December, with his commission in his hand. The authorities there, quite devoted to Cortez, and fully aware that in his fall their fortunes must also decay, threw every obstacle in their power in the path of Tapia. They disputed his credentials, and, by innumerable embarrassments, prevented him from entering the interior.

Cortez, on the other hand, while cordially accepting this important co-operation on the part of his friends, the more valuable since it did not involve him in any responsibility, wrote to Tapia a letter full of expressions of courtesy, and of veneration for the authority of the emperor. The imbecile old man soon became entangled in a labyrinth of diplomacy from which he knew not how to extricate himself. He had not sufficient force of character to cut the tangled threads. It is said that every one has his weak point. Love of money was the great frailty of Tapia. United with this there was great timidity of character. Cortez, with his accustomed tact, discovered the peculiarities of the man, and, with his habitual adroitness, assailed him where his armor was weak. The old man's fears were assailed with threats, and his avarice was approached by bribes, and he very soon capitulated. Re-embarking in his ship, he returned to Hispaniola, leaving Cortez in undisputed authority.

This affair alarmed Cortez exceedingly. The account which he himself gives of it in his dispatch to the emperor is so curious and characteristic of the man, that we must give it in his own words. The dispatch itself will be more interesting and valuable than any narrative we might give of the event. Upon the departure of Tapia, Cortez immediately sent deputies to the emperor with a glowing account of his new discoveries and conquests, with many rich gifts, and the promise of immense future contributions. He gave, as it were incidentally, an account of the mission of Tapia, explained with great naïveté the reasons of its failure, and implored anew that he might be intrusted with the government of the wide realms which his skill and the valor of his followers had attached to the Spanish crown.

"While engaged in this business," he writes, "I received accounts from Vera Cruz of the arrival at that port of a ship, in which came Christoval de Tapia, smelting inspector in the island of Hispaniola. The next day I had a letter from him, informing me that the object of his coming to the country was to assume the government of it by your majesty's command, and that he had brought with him his royal commission, which he should nowhere exhibit until he saw us, but hoped this would be soon. As, however, the horses he had brought were affected by the voyage, he was not able to set out immediately, and begged that we would direct how the interview should take place, whether by his coming here, or by my going to the seacoast.

"As soon as I had received his letter, I answered it, saying that I was much pleased with his arrival; that no one could come provided with an order from his majesty to assume the government of these parts with whom I should be better pleased, both on account of the acquaintance that existed between us, and the neighborly intercourse we had enjoyed together in the island of Hispaniola.

"Tranquillity not being firmly established in this quarter, and any novelty being likely to estrange the natives, I begged Father Urrea, who has been present in all my labors, and who knew well the situation of affairs to the present moment, and by whose coming your majesty's service has been promoted, and ourselves benefited by his spiritual teachings and counsels, to undertake the task of meeting the said Tapia, and of examining the orders of your majesty. Since he knew better than any one what the royal interests, as well as those of this country, required, I requested that he would give such directions to the said Tapia as he deemed most proper, from which he knew I would not deviate in the least degree.

"I made this request in the presence of your majesty's treasurer, who joined his solicitations to mine. He accordingly departed for the town of Vera Cruz, where the said Tapia was; and in order that suitable attentions might be paid to the inspector, either in the town or wherever they should meet, I dispatched with the father two or three respectable persons from my companions, and when they had gone I waited the issue. In the mean time, I employed myself in regulating the affairs of my command, and in such a way as best to promote your majesty's interests, and the peace and security of these parts.

"In ten or twelve days after, the magistrate and municipal authority of Vera Cruz wrote me that the said Tapia had exhibited the orders of your majesty, and of your governors acting in the royal name, which they had treated with all suitable reverence; but that as to the execution of the orders, they had answered that, since the most of the government were with me, having been concerned in the siege of the city, they should be informed of them, and in the mean time they would do whatever the service of your majesty and the good of the country required. This answer, they added, was received by the said Tapia with great displeasure, and he had since attempted some scandalous things.

"Although this answer occasioned me some regret, I answered them, and begged and entreated that they would look chiefly to the service of your majesty, and endeavor to content the said Tapia, giving him no occasion for making a disturbance; and that I was about going to meet him, and to comply with whatever your majesty commanded, and the most your service required.

"As I was now preparing to depart, the members of the council entreated me, with many protestations, not to go, as all this province of Mexico, having been but a short time reduced, might revolt in my absence, whence much injury would be done to your majesty's service, and great disturbance caused in the country. They also urged many other arguments and reasons why it was inexpedient for me to leave the city at present; and added that they, with the authority of the council, would go to Vera Cruz, where the said Tapia resided, examine the orders of your majesty, and perform all that the royal service demanded. As it seemed so essential to our safety that the said councilors should go, I wrote by them to Tapia informing him of what had passed, and that I had authorized Gonsalvo de Sandoval, Diego de Soto, and

Diego de Valdenebro, who were then in the town of Vera Cruz, jointly with the council of Vera Cruz and the members of the other town councils, to see and perform whatever the service of your majesty and the good of the country required.

"When they reached the place where the said Tapia was, who had already set out on his journey to this city, accompanied by Father Pedro, they requested him to return, and all went together to the city of Zempoalla, where Christoval de Tapia presented your majesty's orders, which all received with the respect due to your majesty. In regard to their execution, they said that they asked some delay of your majesty as demanded by the royal interests, for causes and reasons contained in their petition, and more fully set forth therein. After some other acts and proceedings between the inspector Tapia and the deputies, he embarked in his own ship, as he had been requested to do, since from his remaining, and having published that he had come as governor and captain of these parts, there would have been disturbances.

"The coming of the said Tapia, and his want of knowledge respecting the country and its inhabitants, had already excited sedition, and his stay would have led to serious evils if God had not interposed to prevent it. Much greater service would have been rendered to your majesty if, while he was in the island of Hispaniola, instead of coming hither, he had first advised with your majesty. The said Tapia had been often advised by the admiral, judges, and other officials of your majesty residing in the island of Hispaniola not to come into these parts until your majesty had first been informed of all that had taken place here, and on this account they had prohibited his coming under certain penalties, which prohibition, however, by means in his power, looking more at his individual interest than the service of your majesty, he had succeeded in getting removed.

"I have prepared this account of every thing in relation to this matter for your majesty, because, when the said Tapia departed, neither the deputies nor myself drew up any statement, as he would not have been a suitable bearer of our letters; and also that your majesty may see and believe that, by not receiving the said Tapia, your majesty was well served, as will be more fully established whenever it shall be necessary."

While thus engaged, Cortez received intelligence that the province of Panuco was in a state of insurrection. As most of his captains were absent on various expeditions, he promptly placed himself at the head of a force of one hundred and thirty horsemen, two hundred and fifty infantry, and ten thousand Mexicans, and marched to inflict such punishment upon the rebels as should intimidate all others from a similar attempt.

The two hostile bodies soon met. According to the estimate of the Spaniards, the number of the enemy amounted to above seventy thousand warriors. "But it was God's will," the historian records, "that we should obtain a victory, with such a slaughter of the rebels as deprived them of all thought of making any head for the present." Cortez ravaged the country, mercilessly crushing all who offered the slightest resistance. Having thus quenched in blood the flickering flame of independence, he returned victorious to the metropolis.

Here he was informed that some of the inhabitants of the neighboring mountains had manifested a restive spirit, and had caused disturbance in other peaceable districts. Sternly he marched to chastise them. The punishment was prompt and severe; thousands were shot down, and their chiefs were hanged. "They were punished," says Diaz, "with fire and sword; and greater misfortunes befell them when Nuno de Guzman came to be their governor, for he made them all slaves, and sold them in the islands."

The father of Cortez, who was in Spain, and who was a man of much elevation of character, now came forward to aid his son with his influence at court. Implacable enemies were intriguing against the bold Spanish adventurer in the court of Charles V., who had returned from his long absence in Germany, and was now at Madrid. Don Martin Cortez had secured the co-operation of a powerful nobleman, the Duke of Bejar. The young monarch, bewildered by the accusations which were brought against Cortez on the one hand, and by the defense which was urged upon the other, referred the whole matter to a commission specially appointed to investigate the subject. The charges which were brought against him were serious and very strongly sustained by evidence.

1. He had seized rebelliously, and finally destroyed, the fleet intrusted to him by Governor Velasquez, whose authority he was bound to obey.

2. He had usurped powers in contempt of the authority of his lawful sovereign.

3. He had made war upon Narvaez, who had been sent with full authority to supersede him, and had slain many of his companions. He had also refused to receive Tapia, though he was invested with the authority of the crown.

4. He had cruelly, and in dishonor of the Spanish name, put Guatemozin to the torture.

5. He had remitted but a small part of the treasures obtained to the crown, squandering vast sums in schemes to promote his own aggrandizement.

6. His whole system of procedure was one of violence, extortion, and cruelty.

It was urged in defense,

1. Two thirds of the cost of the expedition, nominally fitted out by Velasquez, were defrayed by Cortez.

2. The interests of the crown required that colonies should be established in Mexico. Velasquez was invested with power to traffic only, not to found colonies; consequently, Cortez, in the discharge of his duty, was bound to establish colonies, and to send to the crown for the ratification of the deed, as he had done.

3. It was the wish of Cortez to meet Narvaez amicably; but that commander, assuming a hostile attitude, had compelled Cortez to do the same. The treatment of Tapia was defended as in the dispatch which Cortez had transmitted to the emperor.

4. The torture of Guatemozin was declared to have been, not the act of Cortez, but of one of his officers, who was driven to it by the clamors of the soldiers.

5. It was clearly proved that Cortez had transmitted more than one fifth of the treasure obtained to the crown. It was also pretty conclusively proved that his administration was, in general, characterized by far-reaching sagacity.

The defense was triumphant. Cortez was acquitted, his acts were confirmed, and he was appointed *governor*, *captain-general*, *and chief justice* of the immense empire which he had subjugated. The power with which he was invested was vast—almost unlimited. He was authorized to appoint to all offices, civil and military. He could also banish from the country any persons whose conduct should be displeasing to him. A large salary was conferred upon him, that he might maintain the splendor becoming his rank. His officers were richly rewarded. The emperor even condescended to write a letter to the little army in Mexico with his own hand, applauding the heroism of the soldiers and the grandeur of their chieftain. This was one of the greatest of the victories of Cortez. The depression of his enemies was equal to his own elation. Velasquez was crushed by the blow. He survived the tidings through a few months of gloom, and then sank into the grave, the only refuge for those weary of the world.

When the envoys arrived in Mexico with the decision of the court, they were received with universal rejoicing. Every soldier of Cortez felt that his fortune was now made. But their intrepid commander was not the man for repose. New discoveries were to be urged, new tribes subjugated, and far-distant regions explored. Murmurs loud and deep soon ascended from the disaffected, who now wished to repose from toil in the enjoyment of their wealth and honors. Here is a specimen of their complaints:

"I will now relate," says Diaz, "what Cortez did, which I call very unfair. All those who were the dependents of great men, who flattered him and told him pleasing things, he loaded with favors. Not that I blame him for being generous, for there was enough for all; but I say that he ought to have first considered those who served his majesty, and whose valor and blood made him what he was. But it is useless detailing our misfortunes, and how he treated us like vassals, and how we were obliged to take to our old trade of expeditions and battles; for, though he forgot us in his distribution of property, he never failed to call upon us when he wanted our assistance. When we went to the general with the request that he would give us some part of the property which his majesty had ordered that we should receive, he told us, and swore to it, that he would provide for us all, and not do as he had done, for which he was very sorry. As if we were to be satisfied with promises and smooth words!"

Cortez had a very effectual way of escaping from such remonstrants. He immediately dispatched such men as were troublesome on some important expedition, where all their energies of mind and body would be engrossed in surmounting the difficulties which they would be called to encounter. A man by the name of Rangel, who had some considerable influence, was complaining bitterly. Cortez immediately decided that the distant province of the Zapotecans was in a threatening attitude, and needed looking after. They were a fierce people, dwelling among almost inaccessible cliffs, where no horse could climb and no artillery be dragged. From such an enterprise it was little probable that the troublesome man would ever return. He was consequently honored with the command of the expedition. For apparently the same reason, Bernal Diaz, whose complaints we have just read, was appointed to accompany the detachment.

The forlorn party entered boldly the defiles of the mountains, and wading through marshes, and struggling through ravines, and clambering over rocks, with the utmost difficulty and peril penetrated the savage region. The natives, nimble as the chamois, leaped from crag to crag, whistling an insulting defiance with a peculiarly shrill note, with which every rock seemed vocal. Stones were showered down upon them, and immense rocks, torn from their beds, leaped crashing over their path. Their peril soon became great, and it was so evidently impossible to accomplish any important result, that they abandoned the expedition, nearly all wounded, and many having been killed.

During the period of four years Cortez devoted himself with untiring zeal to the promotion of the interests of the colony. The new city of Mexico rose rapidly, with widened streets and with many buildings of much architectural beauty. Where the massive temple once stood, dedicated to the war-god of the Aztecs, and whose altars were ever polluted with human sacrifices, a majestic temple was reared for the worship of the true God. Cortez erected for himself a gorgeous palace fronting on the great square. It was built of hewn stone. All the houses constructed for the Spaniards were massive stone buildings, so built as to answer the double purpose of dwellings and fortresses.

The zeal of Cortez for the conversion of the natives continued unabated. In addition to the spacious cathedral, where the imposing rites of the Catholic Church were invested with all conceivable splendor, thirty other churches were provided for the natives, who had now become exceedingly pliant to the wishes of the conqueror. Father Olmedo watched over the interests of religion with great purity of purpose and with unwearied devotion until his death. Twelve Catholic priests were sent from Spain. Benighted as they were in that dark age, the piety of many of these men can hardly be questioned. Cortez received them with great distinction. Immediately upon being informed of their arrival at Vera Cruz, he ordered the road to Mexico to be put in order, to render their journey easy, and houses to be furnished, at proper distances, with refreshments for their accommodation. The inhabitants of all the towns along their route were ordered to meet them with processions and music, and all demonstrations of reverence and joy. As they approached the metropolis, Cortez, at the head of a brilliant cavalcade, which was followed by a vast procession bearing crucifixes and lighted tapers, set out to receive them. The Catholic missionaries appeared with bare feet and in the most humble garb. Cortez dismounted, and, advancing to the principal father of the fraternity, bent one knee to the ground in token of reverence, and kissed his coarse and threadbare robe. The natives gazed with amazement upon this act of humiliation on the part of their haughty conqueror, and ever after regarded the priests with almost religious adoration.

When conversion consists in merely inducing men to conform to some external ceremony, while the heart remains unchanged, it is easily accomplished. The missionaries, with great zeal, embarked in the enterprise of establishing the Catholic religion in every village of the subjugated empire. They were eminently successful, and in a few years almost every vestige of the ancient idolatry had disappeared from Mexico.

Cortez did every thing in his power to induce the natives to return to the capital. He introduced the mechanic arts of Europe, and all the industrial implements of that higher civilization. The streets were soon again thronged with a busy population, and the Indian and the Spaniard, oblivious of past scenes of deadly strife, mingled together promiscuously in peaceful and picturesque confusion.

Many colonies were established in different parts of the country, and settlers were invited over from Old Spain by liberal grants of land, and by many municipal privileges.

In the midst of these important transactions, while Cortez was living quietly with the amiable Marina, who had borne him a son, a ship arrived at Vera Cruz bringing Donna Catalina, the wife of the wayward adventurer. This lady, accompanied by her brother, weary of the solitude of her plantation, where she had now been left for many years, came in search of her unfaithful spouse. Cortez made great pretensions to religion. It was his crowning glory that he was the defender of the faith. It would have been altogether too great a scandal to have repudiated his faithful wife.

"Cortez," says Bernal Diaz, "was very sorry for their coming, but he put the best face upon it, and received them with great pomp and rejoicing." In three months from this time the unhappy Donna Catalina died of an asthma. Her death was so evidently a relief to Cortez, and so manifestly in accordance with his wishes, that many suspicions were excited that she had fallen by the hand of violence. Though Cortez had many enemies to accuse him of the murder of his wife, there is no evidence whatever that he was guilty. Cortez had many and great faults, but a crime of this nature seems to be quite foreign to his character. The verdict of history in reference to this charge has been very cordially *Not proven.*

CHAPTER XI.

THE EXPEDITION TO HONDURAS.

THE great object of the Spanish adventurers was to extort gold from the natives. The proud cavaliers would not work, and the natives were not willing to surrender the fruits of their toil to support their haughty conquerors in splendor. Cortez consequently, though reluctantly, doomed them to slavery. They were driven by the lash to unpaid toil. It was an outrage defended only by the despotic assumptions of avarice. The Tlascalans, however, in acknowledgment of their services as allies of the Spaniards, were exempt from this degradation. In all other parts the wretched natives toiled under their task-masters, in the fields and in the mines, urged by the sole stimulus of the lash. The country thus became impoverished and beggared, and masters and slaves sank together.

Cortez had now reduced, in subjection to the crown of Spain, an extent of country reaching along the Atlantic coast twelve hundred miles, and extending fifteen hundred miles on the Pacific shore. With energetic genius which has rarely been surpassed, the conqueror established laws and institutions, many of them eminently wise, for this vast realm.

Cortez had sent one of his captains, Christoval de Olid, to Honduras, to found a Spanish colony there. This intrepid man, giddy with the possession of vast power, and encouraged by the success with which Cortez had thrown off his dependence upon Velasquez, determined to imitate his example, and assert independence of all authority save that of the Spanish crown. But Cortez was the last man to allow *his* authority to be thus trifled with. He immediately sent an expedition under Francisco Las Casas, with five ships and a hundred veteran Spanish soldiers, to arrest the disobedient officer. With pennants flying, Las Casas sailed from Vera Cruz, and was rapidly borne by prosperous gales around the immense promontory of Yucatan, a voyage of nearly two thousand miles, to the bay in Honduras named the Triumph of the Cross, where Olid had established his post. Olid opposed his landing, but, as many of his soldiers chanced to be absent in the interior he could present no effectual resistance.

After a short battle, Olid, hoping for the speedy return of his absent forces, applied for a truce. Las Casas weakly consented; but that same night a tempest arose which wrecked all his ships, and thirty of the crew perished in the waves. Las Casas and all of the remainder of his party, drenched and exhausted, were taken prisoners. Olid exulted greatly in this unanticipated good fortune; and, considering his foe utterly powerless, released the men upon their taking the oath of allegiance to him, and retained Las Casas surrounded with the courtesies of friendly and hospitable captivity. After a time, however, Las Casas succeeded in forming a conspiracy, and Olid was seized and beheaded.

Cortez had heard of the wreck of the ships. No other tidings reached him. But disaster ever added strength to his energies. Vigorously he fitted out another expedition, and headed it himself. Leaving a strong garrison to guard the city of Mexico, and appointing two confidential officers to act as deputies during his absence, he prepared to march across the country, a perilous journey of five hundred leagues, through a wilderness of mountains, rivers, lakes, and forests. Unknown and doubtless hostile tribes peopled the whole region. It was one of the boldest of the many bold adventures of this extraordinary man. He has given a minute narrative of the march in a dispatch to Charles V. Bernal Diaz also, who accompanied the expedition, has given an interesting yet gossiping recital of all its wild adventures.

It was on the 12th of October, 1524, that Cortez commenced his march almost due south from the city of Mexico. His force consisted, when he started from Mexico, of about one hundred Spanish horsemen and fifty infantry, together with about three thousand Mexican soldiers. Apprehending that Guatemozin and the cacique of Tacuba, from their strong influence over the natives, might excite disturbance during his absence, he took them as captives with him. Several Catholic priests were taken to conduct the services of religion, and to convert the heathen tribes. The imperial retinue, for Cortez now moved with the pomp of an emperor, was conducted on the grandest scale the time and the occasion would admit. A large herd of swine followed the army a day's journey in the rear. Most of the food, however, was to be collected by the way.

By the aid of a rude map and Indian guides,

Cortez designed to direct his steps across the neck of the broad peninsula of Yucatan to the head of the Bay of Honduras. For many days their path conducted along a low and marshy country intersected by innumerable streams. Some they were able to ford; over others their ingenious architects would speedily throw a bridge. Occasionally they would arrive upon the banks of a stream so wide and deep that many days would be employed in rearing a structure over which they could pass. Cortez, in his letter to Charles V., enumerating the difficulties encountered, states that in a distance of one hundred miles he found it necessary to construct no less than fifty bridges.

The amiable Marina accompanied Cortez on this expedition, since her services were very essential as interpreter. But Cortez now, having buried his lawful wife, and probably looking forward to some more illustrious Spanish alliance which might strengthen his influence at court, regarded Marina as an embarrassment. He therefore secured her marriage with a Castilian knight, Don Juan Xamarillo. A handsome estate was assigned to the newly-married couple in the native province of Marina, through which the expedition passed on its way to Honduras. We hear of Marina no more. Her son, Don Martin Cortez, aided by the patronage of his powerful father, became one of the most prominent of the grandees of his native land. He filled many posts of opulence and honor. At last he was suspected of treason against the home government, and was shamefully put to the torture in the Mexican capital.

As Cortez and his army advanced day after day through provinces where his renown was known, and where Spanish adventurers were established, he was received with every possible demonstration of homage. Triumphal arches crossed his path. Processions advanced to greet him. Provisions were brought to him in abundance. Bonfires, with their brilliant blaze, cheered the night, and festivities, arranged with all the possible accompaniments of barbaric pomp, amused him by day. He arrived at the banks of a wide, deep, and rapid river. To his great gratification, he found that the natives had collected three hundred canoes, fastened two and two, to ferry his army across. At this place Bernal Diaz joined the expedition. Weary of the hardships of war, he complains bitterly that he was compelled again to undergo the fatigues of an arduous campaign.

"The general ordered," he says, "all the settlers of Guacacualco who were fit for service to join his expedition. I have already mentioned how this colony was formed out of the most respectable hidalgos and ancient conquerors of the country, and now that we had reason to expect to be left in quiet possession of our hard-earned properties, our houses and farms, we were obliged to undertake a hostile expedition to the distance of fifteen hundred miles, and which took up the time of two and a half years; but we dared not say no, neither would it avail us. We therefore armed ourselves, and, mounting our horses, joined the expedition, making, in the whole, above two hundred and fifty veterans, of whom one hundred and thirty were cavalry, besides many Spaniards newly arrived from Europe."

But as they marched resolutely along, week after week, over mountains, through morasses, and across rivers, the country became more wild and savage, the natives more shy, and provisions less abundant. Several days were often occupied in constructing a bridge to cross a river. Scouts were sent out upon either wing of the army foraging for food. The natives fled often from their villages, carrying their food with them. Famine began to stare them in the face. Sickness diminished the ranks, and emaciate men, haggard and way-worn, tottered painfully along the rugged ways.

But the indefatigable energy and wonderful foresight of Cortez saved the army. He seemed to have provided for every emergency which mortal sagacity could anticipate. One day the starving army, almost in despair, came to the banks of a large river. The broad current rolled many leagues through a pathless wilderness, and emptied into the Gulf of Mexico. The army, to its great surprise, found fifty large canoes in a little sheltered bay, laden with provisions, and awaiting its arrival. The river was the Tabasco. At its mouth there was an important Spanish colony. Cortez had foreseen the want at that point, and provided the timely supply.

After resting here for a few days to recruit, the army continued its march, and soon came to a river so wide and deep that they could not bridge it. Here they remained four days, while every skillful hand was employed constructing canoes. It then required four days more for the immense host to be paddled across in these frail barks. The horses swam after the boats, led by halters. Upon the other side of the river they entered upon a vast swamp, extending for many leagues, and tangled by the dense growth of the tropics. They were three days floundering through this dismal slough, the horses being most of the time up to their girths in the morass.

From this gloomy region of reptiles, tormenting insects, and mire, they emerged upon a fertile country, where they found an abundance of Indian corn or maize. But the terrified inhabitants fled at their approach. Foraging parties were, however, sent out to plunder the villages of their stores. They did this efficiently, and the encampment was again filled with plenty. After a halt of three days, the soldiers, having replenished their knapsacks with parched corn, again took up their line of march. Each man carried food for three days. Some of the native chiefs, who had been enticed into the camp, deceived them with the assurance that in three days they would arrive at a large city, where they would find every needful supply. They soon reached the banks of a broad river, deep and rapid. It required three days to construct a bridge to cross it. The knapsacks were now empty. They were hungry and faint, and there was no food to be obtained. Painfully the famishing men toiled along another day, eating the leaves of the trees, and digging up roots for food. Some poisonous quality in this innutritious diet parched their lips and blistered their tongues. To add to their despair, there was no longer any path, and the dense underbrush, with tough vines and sharp thorns, impeded their march and lacerated their flesh. The trees towered above them with foliage impenetrable by the rays of the sun. They were wandering through a dark and dismal wilderness, from which there was no apparent outlet, compelled with sword and hatchet to cut every step of their way through tangled shrubs.

Cortez, guided only by the compass and a rude Indian map, now manifested for the first time deep concern. He could not conceal from his companions the anxiety which oppressed him, for his army was literally starving. He was overheard to say, "If we are left to struggle another day through this wilderness, I know not what will become of us."

Suddenly, to their great joy, they came upon an Indian path. This soon conducted them to a village. The inhabitants had fled, but the

Spaniards found some granaries well supplied with corn. During this terrible march of seven days, many perished by fatigue and hunger. It was also discovered that some of the Mexican chiefs, in their extremity, had seized some of the natives whom they encountered, and had killed and eaten them. The bodies were baked, in accordance with their cannibal customs, in ovens of heated stones under the ground.

"Cortez," says Bernal Diaz, "severely reprehended all those concerned, and one of the reverend father Franciscans preached a holy and wise sermon on the occasion; after which, by way of example, the general caused one to be burned. Though all were equally guilty, yet, in the present circumstances, one example was judged sufficient."

After a few days' rest the army again resumed its march, but pioneers were sent in advance to mark out the way. Their course now lay for many leagues through a low country, abounding in lakes, and miasmatic marshes, and sluggish rivers. The bayous and lagoons were so numerous that most of the communication from city to city was by canoes. The people at first assumed a hostile attitude, but soon, overawed by the magnitude of the force of Cortez, they with great obsequiousness furnished him with all required supplies. Still, it was an exceedingly difficult region for the army to traverse. 'Many days were laboriously employed in bridging the innumerable streams. One wide one delayed them four days, and their provisions were entirely exhausted. Diaz, a man of tact and energy, was sent with a strong party to forage for the famished camp. He returned in the night with a hundred and thirty men of burden heavily laden with corn and fruit. The starving soldiers, watching their return, rushed upon them like wolves; in a few moments, every particle of food which they had brought was devoured. Cortez and his officers came eagerly from their tents, but there was nothing left for them.

But even in this strait, when the soldiers forgot entirely their generals, and even refused to save any for them, they did not forget their spiritual guides. Every soldier was anxious to share his portion with the reverend fathers. It speaks well for these holy men that they had secured such a hold upon the affections of these wild adventurers. Though superstition doubtless had its influence, there must also have been, on the part of the priests, much self-denial and devotion to their duties. Diaz, apprehensive of the scene of plunder, had concealed at a short distance in the rear a few loads for the officers, which, he says, they went and got, with great gratitude, when the soldiers were all asleep.

For eight weary days the army now toiled along, struggling against hardships and hunger. Many were sick, many died, and not a few, in despair, deserted their ranks, and endeavored to find their way back to Mexico. Cortez, knowing full well the heroism of his two captives, Guatemozin and the cacique of Tacuba, was now very apprehensive that they might take advantage of his weakness, incite the natives to revolt, and thus secure his destruction. The peril was so obvious that it must have occurred to every mind. The Mexicans knew that the Spaniards were now in their power, and the Spaniards could not deny it.

Under these circumstances, Guatemozin was accused of having entered into a plot to assassinate the Spaniards, and then to return to Mexico and rouse the whole native population to arms, and drive the invaders from the country. There seems to have been but little proof to substantiate the charge; but the undeniable fact that Guatemozin could now do this, excited to the highest degree the anxiety of the ever-wary Cortez. The stern conqueror, acting upon the principle that the end justifies the means, resolved to escape from this peril by the death of his imperial captive and the Tacuban lord. Cortez accused them of the crime, and, notwithstanding their protestations of innocence, ordered them both to be hung. A scaffold was immediately erected, and the victims, attended by priests, were led out to their execution. Both of these heroic men met their fate with dignity. As the monarch stood upon the scaffold, at the moment of his doom he turned to Cortez and said,

"I now find in what your false promises have ended. It would have been better that I had fallen by my own hands than to have intrusted myself in your power. Why do you thus unjustly take my life? May God demand of you this innocent blood."

The Prince of Tacuba simply said, "I am happy to die by the side of my lawful sovereign."

They were then both swung into the air, suspended from the branches of a lofty tree by the road-side. There are many stains resting upon the character of Cortez, and this is not among the least. Diaz records, "Thus ended the lives of these two great men; and I also declare that they suffered their deaths most undeservingly; and so it appeared to us all, among whom there was but one opinion upon the subject, that it was a most unjust and cruel sentence."

The march was now continued, but the gloom which ever accompanies crime weighed heavily upon all minds. The Mexicans were indignant and morose at the ignominious execution of their chiefs. The Spaniards were in constant fear that they would rise against them. Even Cortez looked haggard and wretched, and his companions thought that he was tortured by the self-accusation that he was a murderer. Difficulties were multiplied in his path. Famine stared his murmuring army in the face. Sleep forsook his pillow. One night, bewildered and distracted, he rose, and wandering in one of the heathen temples, fell over a wall, a distance of twelve feet, bruising himself severely, and cutting a deep gash in his head. Still they toiled along, occasionally coming to towns where there were granaries and abundance, and again, in a few days, as they could carry but few provisions with them, finding themselves in a starving condition. Every variety of suffering seemed to be allotted them. At one time they arrived upon a vast plain, spreading out for leagues, as far as the eye could extend, without a bush or shrub to intercept the sight. A tropical sun blazed down upon the panting troops with blistering heat. Many deer, quite tame, ranged these immense prairies. At another time they approached a large lake of shallow water, and upon an island in its centre found a populous town. The soldiers waded to the island through the clear waters of the lake. They found fishes very abundant, and again had a plentiful supply of food.

Thus far the weather had been fair; but now it changed, and a season of drenching rains commenced. Still, the band, impelled by their indomitable leader, pressed on. They now entered upon a very extraordinary region, where for leagues they toiled through dismal ravines, frowned upon by barren and craggy rocks. The ground was covered with innumerable flintstones, peculiarly hard and sharp, which, like knives, pierced the feet of the men and the horses. In this frightful march nearly every horse was wounded and lamed, and eight perished. Many of the men also suffered severely. The difficulty and suffering were so great that upon emerging from this rocky desert the army was assembled to return solemn thanks to God for their escape.

But now they encountered new embarrassments. The streams, swollen by the rains, came roaring in impetuous torrents from the mountains, and the intervales and the wide-spreading meadows were flooded. One stream, foaming through enormous precipices, emitted a roar which was heard at the distance of six miles. It required three days to throw a bridge across this raging mountain torrent. The natives took advantage of this delay to flee from their homes, carrying with them all their provisions. Again famine threatened the camp. This was, perhaps, the darkest hour of the march. The horses were lame. The men were bleeding, and wayworn, and gaunt. Death by starvation seemed inevitable. "I own," says Diaz, "I never in my life felt my heart so depressed as when I found nothing to be had for myself or my people."

Cortez, however, sent out some very efficient foraging parties in all directions. Impelled by the energies of despair, the detachment succeeded in obtaining food. This strengthened them until they reached a large town called Taica, where they again rejoiced in abundance. The rain still continued to fall in torrents, and the soldiers, drenched by night and by day, toiled along through the mire. Even Cortez lost his habitual placidity of temper and began to complain. The vain and gossiping Diaz would not have his readers unmindful of the eminent services he rendered in these emergencies. With much affected humility he narrates his exploits.

"Cortez," says he, "returned me thanks for my conduct. But I will drop this subject; for what is praise but emptiness and unprofitableness, and what advantage is it to me that people in Mexico should tell me what we endured, or that Cortez should say, when he wanted me to go on this last expedition, that, next to God, it was me on whom he placed his reliance?"

They now arrived upon the banks of a river which led to the sea-coast. At the mouth of this river Olid had established one of his important settlements. A march of four days was required to reach the coast. Cortez, who was entirely ignorant of the death of Olid, and of the overthrow of his power, sent forward scouts to ascertain the state of things, as it was his intention to fall upon Olid by surprise at night. The army moved slowly down the stream, feeding miserably upon nuts and roots. The scouts returned with the intelligence that there were no enemies to be met; that the insurrection was entirely quelled, and the colony, consisting of several scattered settlements, was in perfect subjection to the authority of Cortez. It is difficult to imagine the feelings with which this intelligence was received. Cortez must have felt, at least for a few moments, exceedingly foolish. The Herculean enterprise of a march of eighteen hundred miles through a pathless wilderness, peopled with savage foes, where many hundreds of his army had perished from fatigue and famine, and all had endured inconceivable hardships, had been utterly fruitless. It had been what is sometimes called a wild-goose chase, upon a scale of grandeur rarely paralleled.

They soon arrived at a half-starved colony at the mouth of the river, consisting of forty men and six women. The energies of Cortez were, however, unabated. Foraging parties were sent out to plunder the natives, which was done pitilessly, without any apparent compunctions of conscience, as the hunters of wild honey destroy the bees and rob the hives. Cortez himself set out with a strong party on an exploring tour, and returned after an absence of twenty-six days, sorely wounded in the face from a conflict which he had with the natives. If the natives assumed any attitude of resistance, they were shot like panthers and bears.

Here Cortez built two brigantines, and sailed along the coast some three hundred miles to Truxillo. He established on the way, at Port Cavallo, a colony, to which place he ordered a division of his army to march. Others of the troops were to assemble at Naco, quite an important town, where Olid had been executed. Cortez, upon his arrival at Truxillo, which was the principal establishment of the colony in Honduras, was received by the colonists with great distinction. The Indians in the neighborhood were immediately assembled, and were urged to acknowledge submission to the King of Spain, and to adopt the Christian religion. With wonderful pliancy, they acceded to both propositions. "The reverend fathers," says Diaz, "also preached to the Indians many holy things very edifying to hear." From this place Cortez sent a dispatch to the King of Spain, and also a valuable present of gold, "taken," says Diaz, "in reality from his sideboard, but in such a manner that it should appear to be the produce of this settlement."

Cortez, to his extreme disappointment, found the country poor. There was no gold, and but little food. Worn down by anxiety and fatigue, he was emaciated in the extreme, and was so exceedingly feeble that his friends despaired of his life. Indeed, to Cortez, death seemed so near, that, with forethought characteristic of this enthusiast, he had made preparations for his burial.

One day, as Cortez, in the deepest dejection, was conversing with his friends, a vessel was discerned in the distant horizon of the sea. The ship had sailed from Havana, and brought to Cortez dispatches from Mexico. He retired to his apartment to read them. As he intently perused the documents, his friends in the antechamber heard him groan aloud in anguish. The tidings were indeed appalling, and sufficient to crush even the spirit of Cortez. For a whole day his distress was so great that he did not leave his room. The next morning he called for an ecclesiastic, confessed his sins, and ordered a mass. He then, somewhat calmed by devotion, read to his friends the intelligence he had received.

It was reported in Mexico that the whole party which had entered upon the expedition to Honduras had perished. Consequently, all the property of the adventurers had been sold at public auction. The funeral service of Cortez had been celebrated with great pomp, a large part of his immense property having been devoted to defray the expenses. The deputies whom Cortez had left in charge of the government had quarreled among themselves, and two strong parties rising up, the colony had been distracted by civil war and bloodshed. Every day there was fighting. The natives, encouraged by these disorders, had revolted in three provinces. A force which had been sent to quell the insurrection had been attacked and defeated.

The same dispatches also contained a letter from the father of Cortez, informing him that his enemies were busy, and successful in their intrigues in the court at Madrid, and that two very important colonies in Mexico had been wrested from his command, and placed, by order of the king, under the government of others.

Cortez decided to return immediately, but

privately, to Mexico. His enemies, who had usurped the government, had given out that he was dead. Cortez was apprehensive that, were his return anticipated, he would be waylaid and assassinated. He therefore made arrangements for his friends to return by land, while he privately embarked for Vera Cruz. A violent storm arose, with head winds, and the vessel, after struggling a few days against the gale, was compelled, with shattered rigging, to return to Truxillo. Again, after a few days, the vessel weighed anchor, and again it was compelled to return. Cortez now, in extreme debility of body and dejection of mind, was exceedingly perplexed respecting his duty. "He ordered a solemn mass," says Diaz, "and prayed fervently to the Holy Ghost to enlighten him as to his future proceedings."

He now decided to remain in Truxillo, and to unite Honduras and Nicaragua into a colony which, in extent and resources, would be worthy of him. He dispatched messengers with all speed to overtake his friends, who had undertaken to return by land, and recall them to Truxillo. They, however, refused to return. Again another messenger was dispatched to them by Cortez, with still more urgent entreaties. To this they replied by a letter, stating very firmly that they had suffered misfortunes enough already in following him, and that they were determined to go back to Mexico. Sandoval, with a small retinue on horseback, took this answer to Cortez. He was also commissioned to do every thing in his power to persuade Cortez also to embark again for Mexico.

Though, thus forsaken, he still refused to leave Honduras. Weakened by bodily sickness, which plunged him into the deepest melancholy, his usual energies were dormant. He, however, sent a confidential servant, named Orantes, with a commission to Generals Alvarado and Las Casas, who had returned from Honduras to Mexico, to take charge of the government and punish the usurpers. Orantes performed his mission successfully. The people, hearing with joy that Cortez was safe, rallied around the newly-appointed deputies, and the prominent usurpers were seized and imprisoned in a timber cage. Cortez remained in Honduras until he received intelligence that the disturbances in Mexico were quelled. He now decided to leave the government of Honduras in the hands of a lieutenant, and to return to Mexico. His health, however, was so very feeble that he hardly expected to survive the voyage. He therefore, before embarking, confessed his sins, partook of the sacrament, and settled all his worldly affairs.

It was on the 25th of April, 1526, that the pale and emaciate adventurer, accompanied by a few followers, embarked on board a brigantine in the anchorage at Truxillo. The morning was serene and cloudless, and a fresh breeze filled the unfurled sails. Rapidly the low line of the shores of Honduras sank below the horizon, and Cortez bade them adieu forever.

CHAPTER XII.

THE LAST DAYS OF CORTEZ.

FOR a few days a fair wind bore the voyagers rapidly forward over a sunny sea. They had arrived nearly within sight of the Mexican shore, when clouds blackened the sky, and a tropical tempest came howling fiercely upon them. The light brigantine was driven before the gale like a bubble, and, after being tossed for several days upon the angry deep, the voyagers found themselves near the island of Cuba, and were compelled to enter the harbor of Havana for repairs and supplies.

It was not until the 16th of May that they were enabled again to set sail. After a voyage of eight days, Cortez landed near St. Juan de Ulua. Here he assumed an incognito, and proceeded on foot fifteen miles to Medellin. His aspect was so changed by sickness and dejection that no one recognized him. Here he made himself known, and was immediately received with the most enthusiastic demonstrations of joy. He now pressed forward to the capital in truly a triumphal march. The whole country was aroused, and processions, triumphal arches, bonfires, and music, with the ringing of bells and the roaring of cannon, greeted him all the way. The natives vied with the Spaniards in the cordiality of their welcome and in the splendor of their pageants.

Arrangements were made to receive him at the capital with a triumphant fête. He arrived at Tezcuco, on the borders of the lake, in the evening, and there passed the night. It was now the lovely month of June. The sun the next morning rose cloudless, and smiled upon a scene of marvelous beauty, embellished by all the attractions of hills, and valleys, and placid waters. The lake was alive with the decorated boats of the natives, and the air was filled with the hum of peace and joy. Smiles again flitted over the wan and pallid cheeks of Cortez as the shouts of the multitude, blending with the clarion peals of the trumpet, the chime of bells, and the thunders of artillery fell upon his ear. He immediately repaired to the church publicly to return thanks to God for all his mercies. He then retired to his magnificent palace, and again assumed the responsibilities of government.

The enemies of Cortez were still indefatigable in the court of Charles V., and they so multiplied and reiterated their charges that the emperor deemed it expedient to order an investigation. He was charged with withholding gold which belonged to the crown, of secreting the treasures of Guatemozin, of defrauding the revenues by false reports, and of surrounding himself with grandeur and power that he might assert independence of Spain, and establish himself in unlimited sovereignty.

A commissioner, Luis Ponce de Leon, was accordingly sent by the emperor to assume the government of Mexico temporarily, and to bring Cortez to trial. But a few weeks had passed after Cortez returned to the capital before this messenger arrived. Cortez, surprised by his sudden appearance, was greatly perplexed as to the course he should pursue. The intelligence was communicated to him as he was performing his devotions in the church of St. Francis. "He earnestly," says Diaz, "prayed to the Lord to guide him as seemed best to his holy wisdom, and, on coming out of the church, sent an express to bring him information of all particulars."

After much painful deliberation, Cortez decided to receive the royal commissioner with ap parent courtesy and submission. He sent to him a friendly message, wishing to know which of two roads he intended to take on his approach to the capital, that he might be met and greeted with suitable honors. The friends of Leon cautioned him to be on his guard, for they assured him that Cortez would, if possible, secure his assassination. Leon warily sent word that, fatigued by his voyage, he should not immediately visit the capital, but should rest for a time. Having dispatched this message, he immediately mounted his horse, and, with his retinue, commenced his journey. The vigilant officers of Cortez, however, met him at Iztapalapan. A sumptuous banquet was prepared, and some delicious cheese-cakes were placed upon the table. All who ate of the cheese-cakes were taken sick, and it was reported far and wide that Cortez had attempted to poison Leon with arsenic. There is no proof that Cortez was guilty. The circumstances alone, as we have stated them, awakened suspicion. These suspicions were fearfully increased by unfortunate events, to which we shall soon allude.

Leon arrived in the city of Mexico, and in the presence of all the civil and military officers produced his authority from the emperor,

Charles V., to assume the governorship of the colony, and to bring Cortez to trial. The humbled and wretched conqueror kissed the document in token of submission.

Leon now issued public notice that all who had complaints to bring against the administration of Cortez should produce them. A host of enemies—for all men in power must have enemies—immediately arose. The court was flooded with accusations without number. Just as Leon was opening the court to give a hearing to these charges, he was seized with a sudden and a mysterious sickness. After lying in a state of lethargy for four days, he died. In a lucid moment, he appointed an officer named Aguilar, who had accompanied him from Castile, as his successor. "What malignities and slanders," exclaims Diaz, "were now circulated against Cortez by his enemies in Mexico!" The faithful historian, however, affirms that Leon died of what is now called the ship fever. Notwithstanding all these unfortunate appearances, it is generally believed that Cortez was not abetting in his death.

Aguilar was a weak and infirm old man, so infirm that "he was obliged to drink goat's milk, and to be suckled by a Castilian woman to keep him alive." This decrepit septuagenarian could accomplish nothing, and after a vacillating and utterly powerless administration of eight months, during which time the influence of Cortez was continually increasing, he died. The treasurer, Estrada, by the governor's testament, was appointed his successor. The affairs of the colony were now in a state of great confusion. These new governors were imbecile men, totally incapable of command. The popular voice, in this emergence, loudly called upon Cortez to assume the helm. Estrada, alarmed by this, issued a decree ordering the instant expulsion of Cortez from the city of Mexico. Cortez, thus persecuted, resolved to return to Spain, and to plead for justice in the court of his sovereign. At the same time, he received letters informing him of the death of his father, and of the renewed activity of his enemies at court.

Purchasing two ships, he stored them with a great abundance of provisions, and by a proclamation offered a free passage to any Spaniard who could obtain permission from the governor to return to Spain. After a voyage of forty days he landed on the shores of his country, at the little port of Palos, in the month of December, 1527. Cortez immediately sent an express to his majesty, informing him of his arrival. In much state he traveled through Seville and Guadaloupe to Madrid, winning golden opinions all the way by his courtly manners and his profuse liberality.

Upon his arrival at Madrid, he was received by the emperor with great courtesy. Cortez threw himself at the feet of his majesty, enumerated the services he had performed, and vindicated himself from the aspersions of his enemies. The monarch seemed satisfied, ordered him to rise, and immediately conferred upon him the title of Marquis of the Valley, with a rich estate to support the dignity. Cortez fell sick, and the emperor honored him with a visit in person. Many other marks of the royal favor Cortez received, which so encouraged him that he began to assume haughty airs, and applied to the emperor that he might be appointed governor of New Spain. The emperor was displeased, declined giving him the appointment, and a coldness ensued. Cortez, however, at length regained some favor, and obtained the title of Captain General of New Spain, with permission to fit out two ships on voyages of discovery to the south seas. He was also entitled to receive, as proprietor, one twelfth of the lands he should discover, and to rule over the countries he might colonize.

Cortez was now a man of wealth and renown. His manners were highly imposing, his conversation was rich and impressive, and his favor at court gave him a vast influence. His income amounted to about one hundred and twenty thousand dollars a year. There was no family in Spain which would not have felt honored by his alliance, and when he sought the hand of the young, beautiful, and accomplished niece of the Duke of Bejar, his addresses were eagerly accepted. The storm-worn yet still handsome cavalier led to the altar his blushing bride so glittering with brilliant jewels, cut by the exquisite workmanship of the Aztecs, as to excite the envy even of the queen of Charles V.

Cortez soon became weary of a life of idleness and luxury, and longed again for the stirring adventures of the New World. Early in the spring of 1530, he again embarked, with his wife and mother, for New Spain. With his characteristic zeal for the conversion of the natives, he took with him twelve reverend fathers of the Church. After a short tarry at Hispaniola, he landed at Vera Cruz on the 15th of

July. As it was feared that Cortez might interfere with the government of the country, the Queen of Spain, who was quite displeased that the wife of Cortez wore more brilliant jewels than she possessed, had issued an edict prohibiting Cortez from approaching within thirty miles of the Mexican capital. He accordingly established himself at one of his country estates, on the eastern shores of the lake. His renown gave him vast influence. From all parts of the country crowds flocked to greet him. With regal pomp he received his multitudinous guests, and his princely residence exhibited all the splendors of a court. Most of the distinguished men of the city of Mexico crossed the lake to Tezcuco to pay homage to the conqueror of Mexico. The governor was so annoyed by the mortifying contrast presented by his own deserted court, that he despotically imposed a fine upon such of the natives of the city as should be found in Tezcuco, and, affecting to apprehend a treasonable attack from Cortez, made ostentatious preparations for the defense of the capital.

For a long time there was an incessant and petty conflict going on between Cortez and the jealous government of the colony. At last,

Cortez became so annoyed by indignities which his haughty spirit keenly felt, that he withdrew still farther from the capital, to the city of Cuarnavaca, which was situated upon the southern slope of the Cordilleras. This was the most beautiful and opulent portion of that wide domain which the energy of Cortez had annexed to the Spanish crown. Here the conqueror had erected for himself a magnificent palace in the midst of his vast estates. The ruins of the princely mansion still remain upon an eminence which commands a wide extent of landscape of surpassing loveliness. Cortez devoted himself with characteristic energy to promoting the agricultural and industrial interests of the country. Thousands of hands were guided to the culture of hemp and flax. Sugar-mills were reared, and gold and silver mines were worked with great success. Cortez thus became greatly enriched, but his adventurous spirit soon grew weary of these peaceful labors.

In the year 1532, Cortez, at a large expense, fitted out an expedition, consisting of two ships, to explore the Pacific Ocean in search of new lands. The ships sailed from the port of Acapulco, but, to the bitter disappointment of Cortez, the enterprise was entirely unsuccessful.

The crew mutinied, and took possession of one of the ships, and the other probably foundered at sea, for it was never again heard from.

But the Marquis of the Valley, with his indomitable spirit of energy and perseverance, fitted out another expedition of two ships. This adventure was as disastrous as the other. The two captains quarreled, and took occasion of a storm to separate, and did not again join company. The southern extremity of the great peninsula of California was, however, discovered by one of the ships. Here, at a point which they called Santa Cruz, a large part of the ship's company were massacred by the savages. The storm-battered ships eventually returned, having accomplished nothing.

Cortez, still undismayed, prepared for another attempt. He now, however, resolved to take command of the ships himself. His celebrity induced adventurers from all quarters to seek to join the expedition. Three ships were launched upon the bay of Tehuantepec. Many men crowded on board, with their families, to colonize the new lands which should be discovered. More than twice as many adventurers as the ships could carry thronged the port, eager to embark in the enterprise. In the month of

May, 1537, the squadron set sail upon the calm surface of the Pacific, the decks being crowded with four hundred Spaniards and three hundred slaves. About an equal number were left behind, to be sent for as soon as the first party should be landed at the port of their destination.

Sailing in a northwesterly direction, favorable winds drove them rapidly across the vast Gulf of California until they arrived at Santa Cruz, on the southern extremity of that majestic peninsula. A landing was immediately effected, and the ships were sent back to Mexico to bring the remaining colonists. Cortez did not take his wife with him, but she was left in their princely mansion on the southern slope of the Cordilleras. But disasters seemed to accumulate whenever Cortez was not personally present. The ships were delayed by head winds and by storms. The colonists at Santa Cruz, in consequence of this delay, nearly perished of famine. Twenty-three died of privation and hunger. At length, in the midst of general murmurings and despair, one of the ships returned. It brought, however, but little relief, as the ships which were loaded with provisions for the supply of the colonists were still missing.

The discontent in the starving colony became so loud, that Cortez himself took fifty soldiers and embarked in search of the missing ships. With great care he cruised along the Mexican shore, and at last found one stranded on the coast of Jalisco, and the other partially wrecked upon some rocks. He, however, got them both off, repaired them, and brought them, laden with provisions, to the half-famished colony at Vera Cruz.

The imprudent colonists ate so voraciously that a fatal disease broke out among them, which raged with the utmost virulence. Many died. Cortez became weary of these scenes of woe. The expedition, in a pecuniary point of view, had been a total failure, and it had secured for the conqueror no additional renown. The Marchioness of the Valley, the wife of Cortez, became so anxious at the long absence of her husband, that she fitted out two ships to go in search of him. Ulloa, who commanded these ships, was so fortunate as to trace Cortez to his colony. Cortez not unwillingly yielded to the solicitations of his wife and returned to Mexico. He was soon followed by the rest of the wretched colonists, and thus disastrously terminated this expedition.

In these various enterprises, Cortez had expended from his private property over three hundred thousand crowns, and had received nothing in return. As he considered himself the servant of his sovereign, and regarded these efforts as undertaken to promote the glory and the opulence of Spain, he resolved to return to Castile, to replenish, if possible, his exhausted resources from the treasury of the crown. He had also sundry disputes with the authorities in Mexico which he wished to refer to the arbitration of the emperor. He was a disappointed and a melancholy man. His career had been one of violence and of blood, and "his ill fortune," says Diaz, "is ascribed to the curses with which he was loaded."

Taking with him his eldest son and heir, Don Martin, the child of Donna Marina, then but eight years of age, and leaving behind him the rest of his family, he embarked in 1540 again to return to his native land. The emperor was absent, but Cortez was received by the court and by the nation with the highest testimonials of respect. Courtesy was lavished upon him, but he could obtain nothing more. For a year the unhappy old man plead his cause, while daily the victim of hope deferred. He might truly have said with Cardinal Wolsey,

"Had I but served my God with half the zeal
I served my king, he would not in mine age
Have left me naked to mine enemies."

Cortez soon found himself neglected and avoided. His importunities became irksome. Two or three years of disappointment and gloom passed heavily away, when, in 1544, Cortez addressed a last and a touching letter to the emperor.

"I had hoped," writes the world-weary old man, "that the toils of my youth would have secured me repose in my old age. For forty years I have lived with but little sleep, with bad food, and with weapons of war continually at my side. I have endured all peril, and spent my substance in exploring distant and unknown regions, that I might spread abroad the name of my sovereign, and extend his sway over powerful nations. This I have done without aid from home, and in the face of those who thirsted for my blood. I am now aged, infirm, and overwhelmed with debt." He concluded this affecting epistle by beseeching the emperor to "order the Council of the Indies, with the other tribunals which had cognizance of his suits, to come to a decision, since I am too old to wander about like a vagrant, but ought rather, during the brief remainder of my life, to remain at home and settle my account with heaven, occupied with the concerns of my soul rather than with my substance."

His appeal was unavailing. For three more weary years he lingered about the court, hoping, in the midst of disappointments and intermittent despair, to attain his ends. But at last all hope expired, and the poor old man, with shattered health and a crushed spirit, prepared to return to Mexico in gloom and obscurity to die. He had proceeded as far as Seville, when, overcome by debility and dejection, he could go no farther. It was soon apparent to all that his last hour was at hand. The dying man, with mind still vigorous, immediately executed his will. This long document is quite characteristic of its author. He left nine children, five of whom were born out of wedlock. He remembered them all affectionately in his paternal bequests.

He founded a theological seminary at Cojuhacan, in one of the provinces of Mexico, for the education of missionaries to preach the Gospel among the natives. A convent of nuns he also established in the same place, in the chapel of which he wished his remains to be deposited.

He also founded a hospital in the city of Mexico, to be dedicated to Our Lady of the Conception.

In these solemn hours of approaching death, his conscience does not appear to have disturbed him at all in reference to his wars of invasion and conquest, and the enormous slaughter which they had caused, but he was troubled in view of the *slavery* to which they had doomed the poor Mexicans. With dying hand he inscribes the following remarkable lines:

"It has long been a question whether one can conscientiously hold property in Indian slaves. Since this point has not yet been determined, I enjoin it on my son Martin and his heirs that they spare no pains to come to an exact knowledge of the truth, as a matter which concerns the conscience of each one of them no less than mine."

As the noise of the city disturbed the dying man, he was removed to the neighboring village of Castilleja. His son, then but fifteen years of age, watched over his venerated father, and nursed him with filial affection. On the second day of December, fifteen hundred and forty-seven, Cortez died, in the sixty-third year of his age. He was buried with great pomp in the tomb of the Duke of Medina Sidonia at Seville. A vast concourse of the inhabitants of the whole surrounding country attended his funeral. Five years after his death, in 1562, his son Martin removed his remains to Mexico, and deposited them, not at Cojuhacan, as Cortez had requested, but in a family vault in the monastery at Tezcuco. Here the remains of Cortez reposed for sixty-seven years. In 1629 the Mexican authorities decided to transfer them to Mexico, to be deposited beneath the church of St. Francis. The occasion was celebrated with all the accompaniments of religious and military pomp. The bells tolled the funeral knell, and from muffled drums and martial bands sublime requiems floated forth over the still waters of the lake, as the mortal remains of Cortez were borne over the long causeway, where he had displayed such superhuman energy during the horrors of the *dismal night.*

Here the ashes of Cortez reposed undisturbed for one hundred and sixty-five years, when the mouldering relics were again removed in 1794, and were more conspicuously enshrined in the Hospital of Our Lady of the Conception, which Cortez had founded and endowed. A crystal coffin, secured with bars of iron, inclosed the relics, over which a costly and beau tiful monument was reared.

THE END.

Lightning Source UK Ltd.
Milton Keynes UK
UKOW051941180213

206470UK00001B/128/P